The ROAD BACK TO ME

The ROAD BACK TO ME

Lisa A. Romano

The Road Back to Me
Healing and Recovering From Co-dependency, Addiction, Enabling, and Low Self Esteem.

v2.0 r1.1

Lisa A. Romano Publishing

ISBN: 978-0-578-10268-9

Library of Congress Control Number: 2012902580

PRINTED IN THE UNITED STATES OF AMERICA

"I first picked up the book "The Road Back to Me" to help me deal with some of my own personal demons, primarily because I felt like Lisa had a level of personal insight that far exceeded any person I had ever met. Speaking personally, Lisa's work is both challenging and deeply satisfying because it was exactly what I needed to hear. As a practicing mental health clinician, I find Lisa's work clinically sound and consistent with the most effective evidence based practices. The passion she shares on her web chats are an excellent supplement to her books and I highly recommend them as well."

Kevin L. Petersen PhD, LP, LMHC
Clinical Psychologist/Managing Partner
New Directions Counseling Services

Dedication

I was born to write this story. It has taken me many years to find the courage to author a book that I knew might hurt the people I love the most. It is not, nor has it ever been my intent to harm anyone. In fact, as a child I was very often bewildered by the insensitivity of those I loved. The child I once was, was once too busy deflecting pain to be able to detach from it. As one reads my story, one might come to believe that this book is in some way about vendettas. And if one were to come to that conclusion, one would be wrong.

To My Family:

I love you more than you could ever know. I realize that if you ever actually take the time to read this book, you might be hurt and perhaps even angry. I want you to know that I have been pregnant with this book for many years. Fear of hurting you was the only reason I never had it published sooner. Recently something in me has shifted. I see now that my story can help others who have struggled as I have. Please trust me. This book is not about you. This book is not even about me. This book is about self-love, something the world needs to know so much more about.

To My Childhood Friends:

I would not be where I am today had it not been for all of you. Your open hearts filled me up when I needed love the most. In you I found pieces of my self, and learned to overcome my fear of others.

To My Children:

You have been my greatest teachers. My love for you has been my motivation. My deepest desire is to see joy in your eyes, and to know that you know you are loved. On many occasions I have asked you to trust in me. I know that was not always easy to do. I believe the struggles have been worth the tears. A prouder mother than I, there could never be. You are my heart.

To My Darling:

I realize now that until I found my self, I could not have found you. One of the greatest gifts I have received on the road back to me was the joy of discovering that mature authentic love was real. Thank you for being open to the woman I am. I love you with all of me.

Contents

Introduction to the Lost Self

Time has passed, leaving me with memories now. The subjective has become objective, and in its wake peace has finally arrived. It was not always so. Born into fear, I became it. Unaware, innocent, fragile and new, my tiny being absorbed the oddities of the place I would learn to call home. I could not have known my truth. I could not have known truth. Those who raised me were blind to their own. How then could I have possessed a self? This self, whom I should have known, I did not. Being selfless, detached from the essence of me, resulted in a life I lived in my head. I had to. My world did not see me. Conditioned to believe that my identity was determined by the value others placed on me, life was a maze of constant frustration. This self lay quiet, frozen and still, denied its breath. Beneath the burdens of my every day, my self remained a stranger amidst the valleys so wide. This disconnection within so vast, so deep, it is a miracle it did not swallow me up.

It has taken decades to wash myself of these ghosts called guilt and shame. My childhood, soiled by a haunting sense of unworthiness, has led me down many straying paths. I have known the soothing voice of suicide, and the aroma of death as a welcoming. Pain can splinter souls and leave carcasses as the only evidence that a soul existed at all. I have been a carcass much of my life, although no one could have known that. I learned very early on to disown myself, and to simultaneously smile on cue.

The journey you are about to take, you do so as my companion. I write as the observer now, observing what has been through the jagged peephole of my self-awareness, contentedly unconcerned with the judgments of those who choose to come along for the ride. It is uneasy to remember, as well as to not be able to recall some of what has been. For these reasons I am thankful for the gentle shoulders of wisdom, as spirit urges me to allow uninhibited truths to be told. You will take this stroll down memory lane on the battered bricks that have laid my life's path, and discover how, in the most subtle of interactions, psyches surrender to fantasies and to the silent wills of others, for reasons unknown.

In memory's reflection, it feels as if I have been murdered many times, and -- far more horrifying -- as if my suffering never mattered. Psychological invisibility poisoned my thought process, as it invalidated my experiences large and small. Life was a balancing act. I tiptoed across a thin thread that was strung from one side of my mind to the other, as fate went about its merry way beneath me. Often I wondered if I were real at all.

It is not possible to recover from your own soul's death without regurgitating the bitterness of what has been. A soul's death is the result of invalidation, and the only way to heal is by way of unearthing the ugliness that has been tucked away in the crevices of one's being. A survivor at heart, bizarre coping mechanisms kept me afloat in the cesspools of toxic emotions that flowed through my veins. Ashamed once, I am no more, as the tenderness of self-love blankets me with humble understanding.

I am washed. I am made anew, and it is my deepest desire to help others get clean too. I am not, nor have I ever been worthless. And in spite of all the detours that have been, I have found the road back to me. May you be touched by what you read, for it is this author's most honest recollection. You will experience not only the death of my soul, but the birthing of it as well. Welcome to my heart.

Commandments

My family looked like all the others. We lived in a modest middle-class home in Queens, New York. My brother, sister, and I attended a private Catholic school, and my father owned his own refrigeration repair company, which he managed to operate from our Formica kitchen table. My parents were a handsome couple, and our front hedges were always neatly trimmed. We had a dog named Smokey and a couple of birds, too. During the summer months, it was the norm to find a neighbor or two sitting on our stoop, puffing on a Marlboro, as children littered the dusky streets, catching fireflies.

My mother was a stay-at-home mom. Her days revolved around laundry, ironing, and the cooking of meals that she served promptly at five every evening. My father was a hard-working man who made it home each night just in time for dinner to be served. He adored my mother's cooking, and was not afraid to express his love of food. Mom liked pleasing my father. In fact, she liked that very much.

I am the oldest of three children. I have a younger brother, Marc, and a younger sister, Leslie. Marc and I fought regularly, like most other brothers and sisters I knew who were so close in age. Sometimes the fights got physical. Leslie and I rarely fought, however. For some reason, in my eyes she was special -- angelic, even. Her hair was the color of sunflowers, just like Mom's. And her eyes were as blue as a Caribbean sea. Mom had eyes the color of water, too. Leslie exuded playfulness, and although everyone fell in love the minute their eyes fell upon her, my heart never felt anything but tenderness for my little sister. I was happy she had love.

There were subtle distinctions I secretly wondered about, like if any of the other kids I knew had grandparents and uncles who were alcoholics or compulsive gamblers. Did anyone else my age have a grandmother who had committed suicide, or an aunt with paranoid schizophrenia? Did they have any retarded people in their family, like my Aunt Jane? Beneath it all, I knew my family wasn't like many others, and I knew from the outside no one could have known how different we really were. But these hunches were not ones I felt I could share. You see, in our home we had rules. Rules that were never spoken about, but commandments you followed nonetheless.

I was never told I wasn't allowed to cry, but I was mocked when I did. I was never told I was not permitted to talk about my feelings, but I was shamed when I asked questions, withdrew, laughed, danced, or did not smile when expected to. I was never told I wasn't loved, but I was told I was bad. I was never told I was unworthy, but I was labeled selfish for wanting, for desiring, and for dreaming about having. I was never told I was ugly, but I was never told I was pretty, either. I was told to tell the truth. But instead I always felt we lived a lie.

Pink Elephants

My mother's mother was an alcoholic. Grandma lived directly around the corner from us. The rear of her house faced our back yard. My mother's younger brother Peter lived a few blocks away. He was an alcoholic and a compulsive gambler. My mother's twin brother John never really had a home. He too was an alcoholic and a compulsive gambler. My mother's father, whom I never met, died while my mother was pregnant with me. He was also an alcoholic, and according to Uncle John, he liked to beat up women, too. I would not have known that if it were not for Uncle John. My mother tended to glorify the man who found money to buy himself tailored suits, while his own children dressed in tattered hand-me- downs supplied by empathetic neighbors.

My father's father was an alcoholic. It is rumored that he was also physically abusive to women. According to raw stories told by my father, my grandfather was an explosive drunk who got kicks out of torturing his children when he got loaded. In the clouds of inebriation, he'd find humor in hammering a nail into a piece of wood he'd place on his son's head. He was a volatile man whose rage-filled drunken episodes could not be trusted. My father's natural mother, Pauline, I never met. She committed suicide when my father was only four. My step-grandmother Elizabeth married my grandfather after the suicide. My grandfather was in danger of losing his four children to child services due to his neglect of his children. Elizabeth, a warm, kind-hearted woman, married my grandfather and did her best to weave the family back together. She brought with her a retarded daughter from a prior marriage. Together my grandfather and Elizabeth had a child of their own, named Paula.

My father had three full maternal siblings. His two older sisters were named Maria and Evelyn. His older brother, and the third child of the family, was named Sam. My father was the youngest. Maria detached herself from her family as an adolescent. I never knew her. I have been told she resented Elizabeth as her dead mother's replacement. She severed her relationships with all the members of her family, as soon as she believed she was old enough to do so. I recall sensing the sorrow in my father's voice whenever he spoke of her. He missed the older sister who tried desperately to mother him after their mother's suicide. His sister Evelyn suffered from paranoid schizophrenia, and was in and out of mental hospitals during my childhood. Sam was a large man, who reminded me of a silver back gorilla. He was tall, hunched over, had a protruding jaw, huge skull, and for some reason stared at the ceiling whenever he spoke to you. I tried my best not to look at him very often.

Mom and Dad rarely blended both sides of the family. We'd visit my father's parents on Sundays, and my mother's brothers would stop by during the week, if they stopped by at all. My mother's family wasn't the kind you'd visit, anyway. John never really had a home of his own, aside from the homes of the married women he slept with, and Peter was an undemonstrative man who made it known he didn't appreciate company. My mother's mother wasn't what most would consider the nurturing or communicative type. She was a frail, quiet woman, with stern green eyes, who was wound tightly like a top. I never felt like she was my grandma. This was not a sentiment that ever left my head.

Misfit

Lots of kids lived on my block. Barbara and R.J. were children of my parents' friends who lived a few houses down from our home. R.J. was Marc's friend, and Barbara was Leslie's. If the five of us ever did play together, my brother would be sure to remind me that I was the odd man out, the fifth wheel, the one who had no friends of her own. It would sting like a hot pick to my skin whenever Marc lashed out at me like that. It was so rare that I felt like I fit in. Sometimes I didn't want to remember that I didn't belong.

It was normal for me to spend time alone. During the summer months, while most kids were outside playing together as carefree as the wind, it was most likely that I was in my room daydreaming, writing, or out riding my bike somewhere across town. Experience had taught me that spending time alone hurt less than trying to be accepted. At about the age of ten, I silently surrendered to the idea that I was flawed, broken, bad, and just plain wrong.

Most days I rode my bike to Eaton's Park, where I either fished off of the rocks that bordered the water's edge, or just wandered through the park's trails. I'd pretend not to notice the circles of kids playing handball, or running through the sprinklers. I would pedal past them quickly, wearing a determined look across my face, hoping somehow to make others think that in fact I had somewhere to go. Afraid even of what strangers thought of me, I painted my face with expressions that I hoped would prevent others from seeing how lonely I was.

Sometimes I got to play with Barbara and R.J. when Leslie and Marc weren't around. Marc and Leslie had other friends they played with, and when they were busy doing other things, I'd look forward to hanging out with Barbara or R.J. Their mother Theresa was always considerate of me. I had a hunch she was the one who encouraged her children to come call on me when my brother and sister weren't around. Barbara and R.J. were never cruel to me. In fact, R.J. had a mad crush on me when we were seven. He and I were the same age. The crush didn't last long, and I never appreciated it anyway.

I liked being around Barbara and R.J. There was a bond between them that my own siblings and I didn't have. R.J. seemed truly to care for his younger sister. I remember wishing Marc treated me the way R.J. did Barbara. If Barbara coughed because she had swallowed too much pool water, R.J. would shove walls of water out of his way in a hurry to get to his sister's side. He'd put his arms around her and with great concern in his eyes and in his voice, ask her if she were all right. It was warm, genuine, and left me aching for some of that too.

I perceived Theresa and her husband Joe to be more real than my own parents. When Joe laughed, his entire face and body laughed too. And when he asked me how I was doing, he did his best to get me to stand still long enough to look into his eyes. I knew he cared, but I also knew I couldn't tell him the truth. If I did, he'd listen, possibly address my parents, and then what? It was best I keep the demons locked away. I couldn't articulate them anyway. And more than anything, I didn't want my mother telling me I wasn't allowed to play with Barbara and R.J. anymore.

I Wish I Were a Real Girl

As a kid, I didn't smile much. I never knew that until my mother's friend Connie mentioned it. "You really should smile more often. You should be more like your sister Leslie. She's so sweet. You just look angry all the time," she said, taking me by complete surprise. It made me feel observed, watched, and judged. I didn't like how that felt, and after her comment, I didn't like her very much, either.

I thought I was ugly. I never felt like a pretty little girl. I wasn't a pretty little girl. One time while in Caymen's department store, I was looking at pocketbooks when I heard a sales clerk say, "Can I help you, young man?" My heart sank to the floor as if it were a cinderblock falling from the sky. I felt raw, exposed, and as if my worst fear had been confirmed. I was ugly.

Not long after that incident, I was standing outside of my house when a hairy, older new kid came strolling down our block. He didn't like the way I looked at him, and so he approached me and said, "You got a problem with me?" Before I could get a word out, the kid punched me hard in the stomach, and then hit me in the side of the head as I doubled over, clutching my belly. As I lay on the ground, curled up into a ball, with my arms protecting my head, he kicked me once or twice more before deciding to leave me alone.

I remember feeling stunned and dazed. It all happened so fast. I hadn't done anything to have him pick on me. I didn't even know who he was. I can still see his face in my mind's eye. His eyebrows were black and bushy, and his facial hair seemed abnormal for a kid of thirteen or fourteen. I was only about eleven at the time, and shaken deeply by his violence toward me. I lay on the ground until I was sure he was not going to hit me again. Once he was gone, I slowly rose to my feet, and then scurried to my room bewildered, afraid, bleeding from scrapes to my arms and legs. I never told my parents what had happened. I kept it to myself, and hid in my bedroom, listening from the window to the sounds of all the kids on my block playing manhunt in the street.

A few hours later my brother Marc came to my room looking for me. I pretended to be busy, not wanting him to know how alone I had been feeling. "Lee, did some kid just beat you up?" he asked.

"Well, yeah, some kid punched me outside, but I don't know why. Why are you asking?"

"Because this kid just told me he kicked my brother's ass, and then I said, 'I don't have a brother.'"

I didn't know what felt worse, not knowing why I got beaten up, the pain from being beaten up, the humiliation of being beaten up, or being beaten up by a boy who thought he was beating up another boy. Family dynamics had taught me to swallow negative emotions. There I stood in front of my brother, struggling to take bites out of my shameful reality, doing my best to pretend everything was all right.

I hated the way my mother had my hair cut. She insisted it be kept short. Dorothy Hamill hairstyles were all the rage back then. But the hairstyle did little for my floppy mop of a head. The short layers, which would have looked neatly stacked on shiny straight hair, made my head look like a ball of brown frizz. I was far from a barrette or bow kind of girl, although secretly I wished I were. I was certain the world would have mocked me anyway, even if I ever had tried to look like a real girl. So instead, I learned to tolerate my hair for the mess it was.

I wished I were pretty. In my daydreams I was lovely, beautiful, and dainty, too. I remember wishing that I felt free enough to be the little girl who was buried deep within me. I desperately wanted to feel accepted enough to wear pretty clothes, and to tie my hair back with bows. But the fear of being laughed at by my mother, brother, or peers at school kept me toning myself down, out of fear of having who I really was being rejected by others. Rejecting myself first hurt less.

I remember being called a tomboy. I didn't know what that meant, but I did know it meant I wasn't like all the other girls I knew, or even like my stunning little sister. I climbed trees because it was something I could do alone. I rode my bike and fished, because they too were things I could do all by myself. My scraped knees and scuffed elbows were the result of my trying to make the best out of my feelings of not belonging. They were not representative of who I really was. Who I really was, was a delicate little girl, desperate not to feel like she had to pretend she didn't feel anything at all.

Two Square Pegs/One Round Hole

Aunt Jane was mentally retarded. My grandmother Elizabeth did her best to pretend she wasn't as retarded as she was. In fact, my grandparents allowed my aunt to marry some guy named Paul. Paul wasn't the sharpest tool in the shed, but even I knew my aunt wasn't capable of cooking and cleaning, and I was just a child.

I am guessing that I was about three years old when my aunt married Paul. I remember my grandmother taking me to a store. We went there to buy my aunt a pot roast to cook for dinner. "We're going to help Aunt Jane get ready for dinner sweetheart," my grandmother explained to me. My grandmother and I walked up a long flight of stairs, up into an apartment where Aunt Jane was waiting. She was a short, frail, pasty-looking creature with auburn hair, and eyes that were a mossy green. Sometimes her eyeballs would dart back and forth from side to side. That would always startle me.

Once in the apartment, my grandmother busied herself in the kitchen, while my aunt stood beside her, nervously rocking back and forth. Aunt Jane did that a lot when she got nervous. "Jane, take the pot roast out at five o'clock. Have Paul cut it up. The potatoes should be done at the same time. Remember, Jane, five o'clock -- take the pot roast out at five o'clock," my grandmother instructed, as she took my hand and lead me out of the apartment. "Jane, lock the door behind us," my grandmother continued.

The marriage didn't last. Aunt Jane moved back in with my grandparents into a small bedroom off the tiny kitchen in their home in Maspeth. Her bedroom walls were covered in *Teen Beat* photos of Donny Osmond and Sean Cassidy. She had a small rectangular record player that she played 45's on over and over. She loved music. Music by young men, that is.

She would sit on the edge of her bed in a housecoat, and rock forward and back, forward and back. Her hands would be placed one inside the other, the knuckles of one hand cupped by the palm of the other. She wore penny loafers, and ankle socks. Her skin was always dry. Her hair was usually greasy and unkempt. She had an insatiable sweet tooth, which my parents satisfied each visit with Snickers and Baby Ruth candy bars. She didn't talk much, but when she did, she giggled her way through most syllables.

Aunt Jane liked boys. Although she was probably thirty years old or so, she had the mentality of a very young child. It was puzzling for me at times, to try to comprehend why my aunt was so unlike other adults I knew. A child myself, I could do little more than simply accept this innocent creature for who she was. My grandfather seemed disgusted by the sight of her, while my grandmother seemed to coddle her. My father teased her playfully, and she seemed to like that very much. My mother was kind to her, and many times I witnessed her bathe my aunt, cut her toenails, and trim her hair.

I was about ten when my grandmother would sometimes ask me to walk my aunt to the corner store to get milk. It was then that I first began to realize that not everybody had an Aunt Jane in their family. As we'd walk to the store, we'd encounter stares along the way. Kids would stop riding their bikes just to glare at her, as if she were a freak show exhibit. One time a little boy on a bicycle rode past us as we made our way to the store. As he rode directly alongside us, he said in a voice obviously mocking my aunt's, "Hey Janey, Janey, Janey, Janey. Where you walkin' to Janey, Janey, Janey?"

Anger lit up inside of me as if my legs were matchsticks and the ground beneath me were flint stones. I wanted to hurt him, knock him off his bike, and maybe punch him in his face, but I didn't. Instead, I walked to the other side of my aunt and stood between her and the boy as he steadied himself on his banana seat. "Get the hell outta here before I punch your teeth down your throat," I said to him. My voice was stern, and the look of surprise in his eyes blended into concern as he rode off saying over his shoulder, "Ah, whatever." I didn't even care if he thought I was a boy.

On that day I began to realize something I never had before. In all the differences between my retarded aunt and me, on a deep level she and I had things in common. She didn't fit in. She wasn't pretty. The boys didn't like her. She spent lots of time alone in her room. She fantasized about being loved by a boy. She craved to be loved, accepted, and worthy. She wished she were normal like everybody else, too. But she wasn't. And there wasn't anything she could do about it. The worst part was that others found ways to make certain her feeling of not belonging was something she could never forget.

Speak No Evil

My mother's twin brother was named John. He was named after his father, John Healey. He was my godfather. I never liked him very much, and I knew he didn't like me either. When he'd visit our home, he would often call my brother, sister, and me names. He would refer to us as wise asses, smart asses, pain in the asses, and so on. He had little patience for us, as we would draw my mother's attention from him as he sat at our kitchen table, whining about his unfortunate life circumstances. Uncle John was always in trouble, either with women, loan sharks, or from some effect of alcoholism.

On occasion he would sleep on our living room floor. Homeless, he would take up floor space, watch television all day long, eat our food, and complain when my brother, sister, or I wanted to watch a sitcom or cartoon. He would say things like, "Why don't you kids get the hell outta here already. I wanna watch television. Go outside, go play in traffic will ya, you god damn pain in the asses. Your mother should crack ya one. You kids have no respect for your elders."

One time I will never forget. It sticks with me like gum to the bottom of a shoe on a hot day. He was sleeping on our living room floor. He didn't have money for rent, but managed to buy a gallon of ice cream. There were never many snacks in our house, so opening the freezer to find ice cream was more than a delightful, unexpected surprise. I remember scooping out some ice cream and putting it into a bowl to eat while I watched television. As I sat to watch TV, my uncle looked at me and said, "Who said you could have ice cream? I bought that goddamn ice cream. That ice cream is for me, not you kids." My stomach flipped, and rage built up in me like a suddenly awakened volcano. I wanted to spit the ice cream into his pathetic face. But I didn't. I swallowed it instead.

My parents were forever trying to get him out of trouble. He has been married for a total of five times, and had a child with a woman he did not marry. I have two full cousins I do not know. Over the years I wondered about my little cousin Jason, and my Aunt Catherine. I wondered how they were doing, and why it was we met them only a handful of times. And Alexandra, the pretty young girl he started bringing around when I was about eighteen, and their baby Audrey, they too eventually became ghosts.

On one cold night, I can recall my mother being very nervous. She received a phone call from a man who did not give her his name. She was told to go collect her brother from the sidewalk around the corner. My father scurried to the spot where they had been instructed to find my uncle. He had been beaten so badly that his face was unrecognizable. He was taken to the hospital, where he eventually recovered. I, however, was growing tired of the chaos he consistently brought into our home. And I was growing even more frustrated with feeling like I needed to shrink more and more, because of the issues he forced my parents to focus on.

On my walk to school one morning, a car with two burly men slowed down beside me. The passenger rolled down his car window and stared at me for a while, which made me feel uneasy. Flashing them an angry look, I tried not to look as frightened as I was. "Hey kid, isn't John Healey your uncle?" the passenger asked, as the car he was in kept in pace with me. I pretended not to hear him, and stared straight ahead as I began to walk more quickly, pressing on in anticipation of coming to the intersection at the corner. My heart beating fast, I understood immediately that these were bad men, and that now these bad men knew who I was because of my godfather. I wanted to scream. I wanted to explode, but I knew no one would hear me.

I never told my mother or father about the bad men that followed me that day. I didn't think they'd believe me anyway, and I didn't want my Uncle John to call me a liar. I didn't like how my mother let him get away with pushing me around. My mother would often refer to the missing bond between us as a personality conflict. As a child, I never quite understood what that was supposed to mean. But in my heart, I believed my mom and her brother both felt the same way about me.

"Daddy, Can I Trust You With My Secret?"

I enjoyed drawing when I was a little girl, and so did my father. My dad would take the time to draw with me when Mom wasn't around. When she went food shopping or out to a department store to buy curtains or bedspreads, Dad would sit me on his knee and draw with me. He'd put his right hand over mine and help me sketch things out like barns, or cars, or cartoon characters. He'd explain how to blend colors to make new ones, and how to add shadows where they belonged. I always felt safe there on his lap, unobserved and not judged.

I was about seven years old. Nestled safely on his knee, and with his strong, bare arms cradling my tiny body, I somehow found the courage to unzip my heart. As fear beat the inside walls of my arteries and veins, I said, "Daddy, I don't think Mommy loves me." I wondered what he'd say. I fantasized that he'd look me straight in the eye and ask me why I felt that way. I imagined telling him the way Mommy spoke to me when no one was around. I saw myself telling him that she was rough when she combed my hair, and that she called me a "bad girl" a lot. I envisioned my father swallowing me up, and holding me in his arms. I prayed he'd sit my mom down and tell her he knew how she treated me when he was at work. In my room, while daydreaming, this is the way this story turned out.

As my tiny heart beat, and my little legs squirmed, I tried not to let the tears that were making their way to the corners of my eyes fall and hit the paper my father and I were drawing on. "Lisa, Lisa, Lisa -- don't you ever, ever, ever say that again. Your mommy loves you. See how clean this house is. See how Mommy cooks for all of us. Of course she loves you. Don't ever talk like that again. You're going to make Mommy very mad if you do," he said softly in a disappointed tone, as he gently tapped my scrawny left forearm.

In a flash, my hopes of being heard vanished. I can still remember how the stiffening in my body felt as my mind began to understand that my father was not going to hear what I had to say. My mind swirled into a vacuum, as so many thoughts and feelings surfaced and died, surfaced and died. I worried that I had disappointed my father by telling him my truth. I worried that now he'd tell my mother, and she'd be even more verbally and emotionally abrasive when he wasn't home. I worried about what I was supposed to do with these feelings I had about my mother, too. What was I supposed to do now? I didn't believe Mommy loved me. I couldn't ask her why. She'd call me crazy, or make faces at me, or call me names if I did. My feelings didn't matter. And besides, I was supposed to be grateful.

I couldn't name what I was feeling. All my little mind knew was how jumbled up I felt. When in my mother's presence, all I could feel was a chill, as if the sight of me irritated her. She never hugged me. I can't recall a time when she was ever nurturing, or made herself fully emotionally available for me. As a child I felt like my younger brother and sister, my uncles, my father, his business phones, her cigarettes, her chores, and her feelings all came before me. I felt like I was invisible to her, and in the rare moments when I did feel like she could see me, she could see only what was wrong with me, which always made me feel like I was never enough.

I did well in school. I tried hard to please her by getting good grades. My brother was not the best of students, and I knew that his poor grades upset my parents. To make them feel better, and also to feel validated, I would strive to achieve, in hopes of fixing whatever that feeling was that felt so wrong in my house and in my blood. I would feel perplexed when I brought home an A. My mother's reactions were inconsistent. She'd praise me in front of my father, but on occasion would accuse me of showing off when I presented her with a good grade when my dad wasn't around. I never knew what to expect from my mother, but I knew she wanted my father to believe everything was fine between her and me. I couldn't name these feelings, which always seemed to get bundled up inside me somewhere.

At night, before dinner, my parents would usually talk about the day. On a number of occasions I overheard my mother telling my father that she thought maybe there was something wrong with me. My mother was a tense woman, and cleaned in what most would consider a neurotic fashion. I was little, maybe ten, and she'd ask me to clean, or vacuum. I would do my best, but it was never good enough. She'd inevitably grow frustrated with my attempt at cleaning, and lash out in anger, making me feel wrong for even trying. Her inability to control her frustration would end in a screaming fit, and I was her target. She'd lash out at me, and before long she would go off into tirades about how lazy I was, or how selfish I was. I would feel beaten up and overwhelmed, as if she had sawed the top of my head off and poured all the junk that was brewing inside of her into my being.

At the end of days like these, I'd wind up alone in my bedroom, hiding from my mother's wrath. My brother and sister had lots of friends, so they usually escaped these explosive moments. It was I who was left behind, broken, afraid to make friends, convinced deeply that who I was, was not good -- certainly not good enough. I was not only ugly, but deep within was a flaw so hideous that not even my own mother could accept me. This was the message my inner voice whispered to me often.

My father would rarely respond to the negativity my mother would use to describe me. I don't ever recall a time he spoke badly of me. I wondered if in all those times when my mother tried to get my father to see me in a bad light, if he remembered what I told him on his knee when I was seven. I hoped he did, although a part of me was angry at the man I loved so much, because he did little to protect me from my mother's hidden rage. In my heart, although I could not express these feelings verbally then, on a silent knowing level, I felt as if my father knew that my mother had conflicting feelings for me. I felt as if my father also wanted me to pretend she didn't have these feelings, so as not to rock the boat. My father preferred I not express how I felt, and preferred instead that I swallow the feelings he thought might disrupt his household.

I wrote a poem to my mother once. I was feeling defeated, tired of the bitterness between us. I wanted it to end. I wanted her to know how much I loved her, and that in spite of how angry I made her, and how frustrated I was with her, too, that I saw how hard she worked, how hard she tried to make my father happy, and how hard she tried to fix her brother, too. I saw how kind she could be to Aunt Jane and to my grandparents. I wanted desperately to feel some of the tenderness she bestowed on others. I wanted to feel loved by her, the way her brother did, the way my father did, and the way Aunt Jane did. I wanted to feel like she loved me the way she loved Leslie. She always spoke about how pretty Leslie was. I wanted that. I wanted that love that I knew she had inside of her to scoop me up, and clothe me like a warm blanket. I needed to believe I was good, good enough for my mother's love.

It took courage for me to write the poem. It took even more courage to leave it on her pillow where I knew she'd find it. I waited for her to mention the poem to me, but she never did. The day went on like any other. My mother avoided eye contact with me, as usual. I stayed home all day, hoping she'd open up to me and invite me into her emotionally, but that never happened. Eventually, I mustered up the courage to ask her if she'd read the poem I left for her. I remember how fast my heart was beating when I asked. It felt as if wild horses were running through my chest. "Yeah, but I threw it out," she said. My heart sank, and my mind went blank. I felt short-circuited, as if the wires in my brain fizzled out. I wanted to run, but where to?

I stood there frozen on the staircase for a while, unsure of what move to make next. After a few moments I heard my mother laugh.

"Yes, I read your poem, Lisa," she said, as I wondered why she needed to play these cruel mental and emotional games with me. And that was all she said. She never asked me to elaborate, or thanked me.

"Oh … okay," I mustered. "I just wanted to make sure you got the poem I wrote you," I said, as I awkwardly turned and walked back to my room.

Mom used to say, "Lisa and I have a personality conflict." I never quite understood what that meant, but I assumed it was her way of justifying the lack of a bond of any sort between us. It wasn't that I didn't want one or crave one. It was that I felt wrong for needing or wanting my mother to love me in a way that I could feel like who I was mattered. My mother's energy was repelling toward me. She knew it and so did I. But it was our dirty little secret. From the outside, our family looked perfect, and I had been labeled as far too imperfect to mention my secret feelings to anyone. Who would believe me? What would I say?

One summer, my mother and father agreed to put me in camp. I can't remember if it was my idea or theirs. I do however remember feeling that maybe it wasn't such a bad thought. The idea of being surrounded by kids who didn't know me was as delightful as it was terrifying. I felt stained where I was, and that stain was reflected back onto me whenever I looked into the eyes of those around me.

On the first day of summer camp, a school bus arrived to transport me there. As I walked onto the bus, I remember feeling numb, and as if time had stopped. I stared out the window the entire ride to camp, and never uttered a single word to any of the other kids on the bus that day. I had no idea how the day would turn out. Mentally I existed somewhere on the edge of a cliff, half hoping to fall to the ground below, and the other half hoping to be pulled back and rescued by someone -- anyone.

I entered the program about a month after it had begun. By the time I got to camp, the children had already settled into a routine and had made their friends. I could not help but notice how well they all seemed to get along. They reminded me of peanut butter and jelly. They stuck together in little packs and seemed to be so at ease in one another's company. I however, felt more like a giant infected red toe, terrified of being bumped into, but even more terrified that my infection would go ignored.

It was not easy for me to let my guard down. In fact, I never did. Afraid of everything, I came off as cold, aloof, and perhaps even stuck-up. I am certain the other children perceived me as a big jerk. I found it difficult to talk back when I was spoken to, and found it painfully impossible to extend myself to anyone.

It was all an act, of course. I wasn't the least bit stuck-up. To the contrary, I was plagued with insecurities that made me feel as significant as a single drop of water in an ocean. But how could the other children have known that? And how could I have known that the acceptance I craved would require me to drop the facade I carried? All they saw was a tomboyish-looking girl with a chip on her shoulder. And all I saw was how well I didn't fit in. They could never have known how deeply I wished I didn't feel the need to be so hard. They could have never known how fiercely I wanted to fit in. At the lunch table on that first day, a chubby little girl with an Afro looked at me and said, "You know, if you want people to be your friend, you should really try being nice." I was stunned, and felt my body get even more stiff. She was right. But how could I have been nice? I was ill. I was wrong. On a visceral level there was something rotten about me. I had to protect that truth, otherwise they wouldn't like me. But here they were, not liking me anyway.

That was the first and last day of camp for me. I never went back. So my parents didn't wind up losing the money they spent on me to go to camp, my sister went in my place and had an amazing experience there. This did little more than solidify for my mother and father the idea that there was something wrong with me. I supposed maybe my mother wasn't so wrong for not showing me the validation I craved so much. We had a personality conflict, she used to say. I couldn't fit in, not even with kids who had never met me before. It had to be me. The disease of invisibility was beginning to take me over.

The Seed of Death

My father was the one who told us stories about how my mom and he grew up. Mom rarely offered any information about her past. If my mother wasn't criticizing me, she never found a reason to talk to me at all. If it weren't for my father, I would know nothing about the horrors of her own childhood. My father had a natural need to feel as if his children had some understanding of why he and my mother were the way they were. His stories fit. They made sense, but they often left me feeling guilty and ashamed.

Sadly, my mother was raised in filth and squalor. My father said he had never seen a cockroach or a mouse until he visited my mother in Corona Queens while they were dating. He told of being shocked by the obviously neglected furniture, and the tears in the carpets that lined the small rooms. He'd recall how the apartment was infused with the stench of alcohol, and reminded us that every member of my mother's family was an alcoholic, except her. The apartment my mother lived in was located above a bar.

"Your mother used to have to go get her mother off of a barstool downstairs, because her mother was too drunk to make it back to their apartment. Your mother would clean her up and put her to bed. She was only a little friggin' kid. Your mommy is a good woman, so be good to your mother," he'd say to my brother, sister, and me.

My father made certain to let us know why my mother had the compulsion to clean as often as she did. He told us we should be happy and grateful that Mommy cleaned so much. He said that she yelled at us because she wanted a clean home. He said that she loved us, and that's why she cleaned so often. He told us not to make her angry. She was doing her best to love us. He told us not to be selfish, and to leave her alone.

Even as a small child, I was somehow able to comprehend why my father painted such a sorrowful picture of my mother's childhood for us. I would inevitably feel sorry that my mother had to endure what she had as a little girl. I wished she would let me hold her hand, or hug her, or let me do something nice for her. But I knew that closeness was not as much as a priority for her as it was for me. Mom spoke to me only when she had to. Her soul was a stranger to me.

My mom did everything barefoot, including mopping the floors with bleach and water. Her feet were dry and her heels bore signs of hard labor. Once in a while one of our neighbors from down the street asked me to watch her kids while she went to play bingo at our church. She was a generous woman, and often paid me extra if she won big at bingo. I remember saving money up to buy my mother a new pair of sneakers. I remember hushing my doubts away about buying her a present. My little hope spot told me Mom would be grateful, and appreciative that I cared about her weathered feet. Then she'd know how much I loved her, and maybe, just maybe she'd reflect back to me some love, or a sense of acceptance in her eyes. Maybe then she'd know I wasn't all bad. Maybe then I'd know that, too.

I remember my mother looking down at the box with a puzzled look on her face. It wasn't the look I was hoping for. When she opened the box, she looked up at me with a sarcastic expression and said, "Whattya think, you can buy my love, Lisa?" Speechless, my little heart felt dazed, as if I had done something wrong or even bad. Self-doubt, guilt, and even shame enveloped me. These were familiar feelings.

No matter what I tried to do to gain my mother's acceptance, it always failed. Nothing was more important to me than gaining her love, when I was a little girl. Feeling invisible to the being who created me felt unnatural, ill, and rotten. Being so immensely void of any feeling of worth, and simultaneously engulfed by fear, ate me alive from the inside out. My mother, my source of life, could not accept me, and worse, in front of others she pretended she did. My awareness of the contrast in realities swept me up in tidal waves of confusion. My states of being were so unsettled, so mind-blowing, so subjective ... life almost swallowed me up.

In my tiny little heart I kept a tight grip on the idea that one day Mom and I would feel connected, and I would finally know what belonging felt like. On one of those rare days when hope took me over, I rode my dark-blue 10-speed Schwinn to the card store down on Main Street. I remember mulling over the cards one by one. I was searching for the perfect one that would put into words what I did not have the courage to say to my mother face to face.

I found a card that said all the things I needed to say. It was a card full of mushy emotions I wished I could share with Mom. It was a card that expressed how much the recipient was loved and appreciated. I made it all the way to the counter to pay for the card, when a piercing negative thought entered my mind. Filled with self-doubt, I turned, and walked toward the rear of the store to slip the card back into its slot.

I didn't leave the store empty-handed. I bought myself a bag of garlic and onion chips, a king size Charleston Chew, and a can of Pepsi instead. I held the brown bag full of junk food close to my side as I rode off down Main Street, heading toward the park. On the way there, I remember the wrestling match that was going on inside my head. I heard the voice of self-doubt tell my little drop of hope, that I was bad. I was not a good little girl. Only good little girls gave their mothers cards like that, I thought. It was impossible for me to be capable of being kind. My mind twisted and turned until it finally cried Uncle.

I find myself not wanting to remember that day. As if it were yesterday, I can visualize clearly where I was the moment I gave into the feeling that I was bad. I felt stupid and even embarrassed for myself to myself, that I had had such a crazy thought in the first place. The tornado of emotions twisted and turned within me as sadness, shame, and guilt chimed along.

We're Not in Kansas Anymore

I called him Uncle Ronny, the short stout man who stood beside Aunt Evelyn. He was always smiling and joking with Aunt Evelyn. She was a beautiful woman with blonde hair and green eyes. I remember thinking that maybe her teeth were too big for her smile.

They were nice to me. I looked forward to them coming to our house, although that wasn't very often. They gave me a gold ID bracelet for my birthday. It was a delicate piece of jewelry, and it had a small diamond in it after my name, which was written in script. I still remember unwrapping the gift and thinking to myself, "Is this really for me?"

My father was a jokester. His merriment, however, usually came at others' expense. But because all who knew him understood that his intent was not malicious, the puns were absorbed well and any sense of bruising faded quickly amongst roars of laughter. His relationship with his sister Evelyn was fun-spirited. She seemed to enjoy her brother's good nature and natural lead as family entertainer. Her laugh was hearty, and so was Uncle Ronny's. From my position, this childless, well-groomed couple was the picture of happiness. Many times I wondered if I could ever be as well-dressed and happy as Aunt Evelyn.

My father had taken me to their apartment only a handful of times. It impressed me. It was neat and warmly decorated, as if by design. You got the sense that money was not a concern. I enjoyed the feeling I got when I was there. It was as if she had made something of herself, and she wasn't afraid to dress her home in a way that pleased her. My aunt worked in Manhattan. Back then, that was a big deal. She wore tailored clothing and high heels. Her fingernails and toes were always manicured. Many of her traits were unlike my mother's. Being around Aunt Evelyn helped breathe the concept of possibility into my ever-forming thought process.

Because I liked going there so much, I was excited when my father ordered my brother Marc and me into his blue Volkswagon van. "Marc, Lisa...get in the van. We're going to see Aunt Evelyn," he shouted.

Dad seemed uneasy as we drove to his sister's apartment in Forest Hills. I stayed quiet, waiting for him to begin talking. That was usually the way it was when I was around my parents. I spoke only in response to something they said. I was so fearful of being criticized, embarrassed, or shamed for something that I might offer voluntarily, that it became normal for me not to say anything. I wanted to ask him why he seemed so nervous, but I had been programmed not to upset my father, especially when he was irritated.

"Goddamn it, goddamn it, goddamn it....ahh, shit. Now what? Now what?" my father began to chant, his fist smacking the sides of the steering wheel. "Look, you guys, we are going to Aunt Evelyn's apartment because her landlord just called and said she is going crazy. She is screaming and throwing things around her apartment. She won't let her landlord in, and he doesn't know what's going on. I am taking you guys there because maybe if she sees you she'll calm down," he said.

I had never seen my father so irritated before. Not like this, anyway. My father was more of an up and down tense kind of man. When he was in a good mood, he was in a really good mood. It was the same with anger. This generalized anxiety and tension showed a new side of my father. I could tell he was intellectually concerned. Whatever was happening with his sister worried him deeply, and thus made my belly turn inside out.

My aunt came to the door in a robe. Her face was not on. She had pink fluffy rollers hanging from various strands of hair from her head. She welcomed us in. Her aura was chaotic. Her speech was swift. Her body movements were constant. I didn't know this woman.

My father took cool control. With calm in his voice he said, "Evelyn, how you doin'? Is everything all right? What happened to your arm, Evelyn?" The inside of one of her forearms was bright red and blistered.

"Ross, they came right through the television. Starsky and Hutch came right through the television, grabbed me, dragged me to the stove, turned the burner on, and held my arm over the flame," she said.

I was confused, and growing increasingly more anxious as time ticked. Without making excuses, I went into my aunt's bathroom. It was right off the kitchen. I slowly shut the door behind me, and immediately felt guilty that I had left Marc out there, with them. I imagined opening the door a crack and motioning for him to come hide with me, but I was afraid I'd upset my father or my aunt further. I slumped to the tile floor, my back swiping the wall on its way down, and sat there until my father called my name to come out.

On the way home, I kept waiting for my father to ask me why I had been in the bathroom so long. He never did. He was too distracted by what was happening with my aunt. He told Marc and me that Aunt Evelyn was very sick. "I think Aunt Evelyn has paranoid schizophrenia," he said. I had no idea what that meant, but I knew what the word paranoid meant, and I had heard the kids in my class use the word schizo before. I knew whatever paranoid schizophrenia was, it wasn't good.

My heartbroken father was the one who drove my aunt to the mental hospital. My father was right. She had paranoid schizophrenia. I remember eavesdropping on the conversations my parents had at the kitchen table about Aunt Evelyn. From the spying, I learned the awful truth. As it turned out, the man I called Uncle Ronny wasn't my uncle after all. In fact, he and my aunt were never married. Ronny was living a double life. When he wasn't with my aunt, he was with his wife and their three children. When my aunt discovered the truth, it destroyed her psychologically. She was unable to process the reality and the subsequent mudslide of emotions that followed. The doctors told my father that her mind simply split, and now she could trust no one, not even characters on television.

Ronny was a bus driver who drove for the City of New York. He told my aunt he was doing overtime or swing shifts, when he couldn't make it back to their apartment they shared. She believed him. She had no reason not to. Ronny told his wife the same stories he told my aunt. She too believed he was a workaholic. We all did.

I missed Aunt Evelyn, the one who always smelled so pretty and wore such fashionable clothing. I missed daydreaming about growing up to be just like her. I missed seeing her and Uncle Ronny together. They were fun to be around. They seemed so happy. And I missed Uncle Ronny -- or shall I say Ronny -- too.

Wants Not Allowed

My father was a very hard-working man, and my mother was a very hard-working woman. All my parents ever did was work. They were forever busy with this thing or that. Something always had to get done. Time was meant to be filled up. Anxiety was the air we all breathed. My parents could never have known that in all their fussing, and in all their distraction-seeking, in essence they were conditioning their children to be comfortable with angst.

Money was a hot topic in our house. My father kept a tight grip on his wallet, and an even tighter grip on my mother's. My brother, sister, and I knew not to ask for money. In truth, we knew not to ask for anything. Asking was frowned upon. We were encouraged not to ask, and lectured if we did. I'd be confused, because every once in awhile I would hear my dad talk about placing a bet down at OTB, the off-track betting place not far from our home. He never went alone. Usually Uncle John was riding shotgun.

Mom didn't like the gambling. Often, in a passive-aggressive way she'd slide a negative comment into a conversation she was having with my Uncle John and dad. She was clever. She knew just what to say, and how far to go, before Dad would blow up. "Funny. Ross...I thought we were living on a budget? Are you sure you wanna go to OTB with my brother?" is a phrase she'd use. My father didn't appreciate being challenged. His responses varied based on the degree of my mother's sarcasm. If she hit a particular nerve, my father's demeanor would stiffen. His back would get straight as he aligned his spine almost as if to defend himself, and dart an intimidating glare at my mother.

"Ya know...I hate when you do that shit, Gloria," he'd say.

My parents never had arguments. They played mind games instead. It seemed as if each of them was in a constant battle to remain in control. When my mother was upset with my father, she'd go as far as to get sarcastic, and then pull back. And when my father was upset with my mother, he'd shake his finger at her, and say something like, "Okay -- that's enough, Gloria," in a demonstrative voice, and then the whole thing would get swept under the rug. The day or the night would go on as if nothing happened. But something did happen. It was just in the air now.

My mother was my father's secretary. She answered his business phones, and booked appointments for my father. He was an entrepreneur – a good one, too. My mother didn't get a salary for the work she did for my father. I doubt it was ever even considered. Speaking up for herself was not on my mom's radar. She simply did what was needed. My mother had an uncanny ability to sense my father's needs. Before herself, she always did for him.

My mother was frugal. She had to be. She had no other choice. With whatever money my father gave her to go food shopping each week, she somehow managed to do an amazing job at spreading the cash around. Mom cooked every night, and not just hotdogs and beans. Looking back, I find myself proud of how masterful she was in many regards. Void herself of any motherly love, or fatherly protection, my mom somehow made it possible to handle my father's controlling personality, run a meticulous home, and undertake well-balanced meals every evening. I was not a child unaware of the good in the woman who could find no good in me, her child.

Mom didn't have the things she deserved. She didn't have nice clothes, or nice shoes. She didn't own fancy jewelry and would never even dream of paying to have someone else polish her fingernails. I always felt that there was a little girl in her trying to be good enough, too. As if she were glass, and as if my heart had sight, I could see in her eyes, and in the way she moved about my father, that she was begging to be seen. My heart believed she cleaned, cooked, and pinched pennies in an attempt to make my father proud of her for being such a good little girl. I learned to watch from a distance how tuned-in my mother was to my father's expressions of satisfaction as well as dissatisfaction. It was as if her reading of him guided her moment by moment. My body, mind, and heart would ache for her, as within me resonated loudly the replica of the vibrations she oozed for my father, that I oozed for her.

I cannot claim that my parents were monetarily selfish. Neither of them spent money on themselves for "things" that were not considered a necessity. Clothes and shoes were considered essential, and never ornamental. We all settled, including my parents, for the basics. The theme in our house was clear. Don't want, ever, and if you do, don't ever admit it. Pretend to be grateful for what you have, even if what you have been given, you hate.

I see now how fear riddled both of them throughout their lives. My father, so plagued by the taunts of failure, clamped down on his money, in an attempt to hush the demons called "not enough-ness" liked to shout. My father saw money as a "thing" that made him believe in his worthiness. Although my father has always claimed that he was not affected by his mother's suicide, my heart's higher self tells me a different story. My father is not a giving man. He is as stingy with his emotions as he is with his money. And under the circumstances that affected his early life, it is not difficult for me to understand how this can be so. I always wondered if the fear of not having money was in some way linked to his fear of being left alone, as he was when his mother stuck her head in an oven when he was four.

It is required of me as an author to tell the entire story to the best of my natural ability. And so, while all I have revealed is true, it is also true that there were moments, although far and few between, when my parents somehow found the money they needed to do something that very well might have been considered unnecessary to many others. My brother, sister, and I had had orthodontic treatment since we were very young. My father paid for his own medical insurance, but did not have a policy that covered dentistry. This meant that all the braces, retainers, and tons of office visits to dentists and orthodontics had to be paid out of my father's pockets.

I knew my mouth was important to my parents. Unfortunately, when you are young and suffering from the pangs of emotional invisibility, it is all but impossible to correlate excellent dental care with parental love. As an older and wiser observer of my past, however, I can bridge that gap and find in it a sense of worthiness I could not access when I was a child. My mouth was so important to my parents, that when I was sixteen, they paid to have my jaw surgically corrected.

I can recall my mother telling one of her friends that she was the one who insisted to my dad that my brother and I both have the surgery. She said there was no way her children were going to have jaws that were out of alignment, or who had crooked teeth. When I was a child, I wondered if my bad jaw was the reason Mom and I didn't get along. I wondered if she resented the money she spent on taking me back and forth to the city, or on braces, or retainers. I wondered if we'd get along better when I had straighter teeth. It was impossible for me, then, to comprehend that possibly this was the way my mother showed me she loved me.

Smile for the Camera

It was a hot August afternoon. Marc and Leslie were off busy with other friends. The phone rang. I was listening to music in my bedroom when Theresa called. R.J. and Barbara wanted me to go swimming with them in their pool. Theresa called to invite me over. Excitedly I jumped off my bed, grabbed a towel from our bathroom, and ran across the street, anxious to be the third wheel, opposed to the usual fifth.

I always felt freer when my family wasn't around. I felt especially carefree at Theresa's house. Their home wasn't immaculate like ours. It seemed as if Theresa's husband Joe was forever starting and never finishing a new household project. I can still see the unpainted sheetrock hanging in their living room, in my mind's eye. Theresa's kitchen was always in disarray. Pots and pans filled her kitchen and cluttered her stove. It may have been cluttered with stuff, but the air was free from static, and there were never any pink elephants sitting in the living room.

Barbara, R.J., and I were jumping in and out of the pool, just having a good time. We were diving for pennies and having relay races. I remember wishing for more of the anxiety-free moments I had when I was with R.J. and Barbara. I remember wishing that Marc weren't so mean to me when we were all together. And I remember wishing that I were Barbara's age and that Leslie were the big sister instead of me. If I had been the youngest child, then Barbara would have been my friend, my real friend.

Not long after I got to Theresa's house, Theresa yelled to me through her kitchen window screen. "Lisa, your mom just called. Her friend Lucey Ann just stopped by your house, and all her kids are in your pool. Your mom wants you to go play with them now." I was not the kind of child who could pretend. If I was not happy, it was impossible for me to act as if I were. When I was unhappy, it was obvious, which was most of the time. With Theresa's request came a surge of anger, as well as fierce resentment. I immediately understood what this was about, and I wasn't about to pretend I didn't.

I asked Theresa if I could come right back once I went to see what my mother wanted, and she said yes, but that it would have to be okay with my mom. I begrudgingly jumped out of the pool, grabbed my towel, and ran across the street, hopping the whole way, doing my best not to let the skin on the bottoms of my feet rest upon the scorching slate sidewalks for longer than necessary.

I deliberately entered our house by the front door. I assumed my mother would be in the backyard with Lucey Ann and her kids. As I walked through our tiny hallway and into the kitchen, I could hear the sounds of children playing. Lucey Ann had six children of varying ages. "Mom, what do you want?" I asked her through the screen in our back door. With a huge smile that was unfamiliar to me, my mother, in a just as unfamiliar a gentle tone, said, "Oh there she is. Lisa, say hi to everyone. Lucey Ann brought all her kids over to go swimming."

Without uttering words to one another, my mother and I knew we were headed for a showdown. I knew why she wanted me home now. I knew she'd interrupted the rare time I had alone with R.J. and Barbara just so that I could make her look good in front of her friend Lucey Ann. My mother expected me to entertain Lucey Ann's children for her. "Hi," I said, and then turned away from the screen, as I made my way back down the tiny hallway and out the front door.

I hadn't made it off the stoop before I felt my head full of wet hair being yanked from behind me. Then within seconds I was being pelted by the back of a pink Avon brush. My mother pulled one of my arms over my head, and held me close to her as she hit me with the other hand, which held the Avon brush. I was dazed, in pain, embarrassed, and with every blow, I grew more angry at my mother. I was not her puppet, I thought, despite how marionette-like I appeared as my feet danced to the beat of the pain that rhythmically ran down my bare wet back. I had made her just as angry as she had made me, but in her violence she made it clear who the winner in this showdown was going to be.

I refused to cry. I refused to let her see me cry, and as she continued to beat me on our front stoop, and as she repeated the words, "How dare you embarrass me," over and over, syllable by syllable, beating my body as if beating a drum, I melted into the pain rather than fleeing from it. At least the pain was real.

Nowhere to Hide

I remember my soul's ears perking up at the sound of my mother's laughter. She sounded as if someone were tickling her ribs from the inside out. I was immediately anticipating the idea that perhaps in her moment of folly, she might find herself less resistant to me. Hoping to be sucked into her by her joyful vibrations, I placed my school backpack on the back of a kitchen chair and began slowly walking up the staircase that led to the bedrooms in our house.

Mom didn't know I was home or that I was making my way up the stairs. I could tell by the consistency in her laughter. As I neared the top of the landing, I could hear my brother Marc's voice. He had stayed home that day. He claimed he was sick. With every step I took, Marc's words became clearer. At about the third step from the landing, my heart froze. Stunned for a moment, I listened intently to the words that were falling from his lips. The words that floated in the air were familiar. They were my words.

I had been keeping a journal since I was seven years old. I was now about eleven. Ink helped to carry out of me all the thoughts and feelings that would otherwise have gobbled me up. Paper never mocked me or ignored what I had to say. Writing soothed the beasts in me, and helped me not to feel so alone. My saving grace, journaling was the one thing I did that I believed my mother would be unable to judge or dismiss. My thoughts were all I had in a home that made me feel more like a bacterium in a petri dish than an innocent child.

My mother questioned everything I did, or didn't do. In the morning before school, she'd say something like, "You're going to school… like that?" as if to insinuate I didn't look right, or good enough. It was the norm for my mother to pummel me with questions. They weren't questions filled with motherly concern. They were questions of an interrogating nature, which had a way of making me feel as if I were being questioned about a crime that had been committed. "Why did you do that?" "Why did you go there?" "Why didn't you do that?" "Why didn't you go there?" These were the kinds of questions she'd ask about the most mundane things; the questions made me feel lost within my own mind. They were maddening, nonsensical, and crazy-making.

Once, in front of my brother, sister, and father she asked, "Lisa, have you been changing your underwear. It's not nice to smell, you know. I can't find your underwear in the laundry. I hope you aren't going to school like a piggy girl. You wouldn't want anyone talking about how you smell, would you?" Comments like these were the norm. Emotions would spring up like rapid fire in my mind, as I did my best not to buckle under the enormity of the barrage of embarrassing innuendos. My mother had a way of peeling back my skin, and dripping acid into my exposed flesh. But because her assaults left no physical evidence, my pain was considered unreal, and invalid. I would be reduced to a toxic oasis, left alone to lick my own wounds.

When reality hit me on the staircase that day, and my mind grabbed hold of the fact that my mother and brother were laughing at my secret feelings, rage enveloped me. It was hard to keep breathing. I leapt to the top of the landing and skipped the final three steps, in a hurry to end the violation they had begun of my hidden thoughts. I ripped the journal out of my brother's hands, and began to unravel in front of them both, practically crippled not only by their insensitivity, but by the reality that my mother was not going to sweep me into her after all. Her joy was the result of her finding humor in what I had written in secret. Her exposure of me was what was tickling her from the inside out, and what was stabbing at my soul from within.

As I struggled to stay on my feet, with tears soaking my uniform blouse, Marc and my mother continued on with their laughing. "Oh, stop, Lisa. What are you crying about? So we read your journal. What's the big deal? You better relax. You're looking crazy right now. Wait until your father gets home and I tell him how crazy you acted just because we read your journal," was her response. Marc chimed in, and tossed a few dynamite sticks of his own on my already flaming wounds. The two of them, like two schoolyard bullies, left me alone in my room to deal with the havoc they created, mocking me as they walked down the stairs, griping to one another about my "psychotic" reaction.

As I teetered on the verge of adolescence, my tolerance of my mother's intolerance of me began to wane. Once a tiny, innocent child starving for her nuture, I was now slowly growing resentful of her passive-aggressiveness and her constant invalidation of the emotional, psychological, and intellectual being I was. I was tired of being the whipping post, and even disgusted by her insensitivity as well as blatant disregard for my mind, my body, or my soul. In her eyes, I knew that I -- whoever I was -- didn't matter. It was impossible for this woman whom I called "Mother" to "see" me, to consider my feelings, by seeing past her own. Her wounds were too deep. Her mind was too locked. Her heart had turned cold long ago.

How Far Can I Run?

I ripped my journal into shreds that day. It was my way of saying, "Hey, Mom; hey, Marc -- fuck you! Now you'll never know what I think. Now you'll never be able to hurt me. Because now I will never let you again." I was so angry that I stuffed the torn pages into my backpack, instead of putting them in our trash. I was afraid she'd go through the pieces and tape them back together. I felt like my mother was everywhere.

I told myself my writing was over. I told myself there was no safe place. I walked on eggshells as a child. I am not sure if Marc or Leslie felt that way. I have specific memories of thoughts like, "Okay, it's been three days and I haven't been attacked yet. The house hasn't exploded in a while, so I'd better be on the lookout because I know it's going to happen soon." My parents never knew it, but I felt like living in that house was like trying to live a childhood on a mine field. My mother was unaware of how unhappy she was, and that she had either psychologically projected her abusers' abuse of her onto me -- or perhaps she was simply playing out the lack of connection with me that she felt between herself and her own mother. My father was simply a workaholic, who could not deal with conflict. Who was I to turn to, then, with my soul's hemorrhage?

For a short while after my mother read my journal, I found refuge in the cocoon of anger. I would come home from school and hide away in my room. I would complete my homework away from my brother and sister, but especially away from my mother. And when I was done, I would lie on my bed, close my eyes, and talk to myself inside my own mind. It was difficult, however, to keep my anxiety under control. The inability to "get out" what I was feeling inside, was taking its toll on me psychologically. I missed my pen.

I avoided my mother at all costs. I refused to look at her, or answer her questions with more than one word. I had been stripped of any sense of power or control over my life by her, and she was enjoying the results of her torture. My withdrawal from her only solidified her characterization of me, however.

I was so disgusted by the sight of my brother and mother that I didn't even want to eat dinner at the table with them at night. I knew this would be a sticking point with my father, because seeing us all around the table somehow made him feel like everything was cohesive in our home. The night my mother read my journal, she painted a gruesome picture of my reaction to my dad. I was permitted to skip dinner that night, but tomorrow would be a different story.

Ornery, and still suffering the sting of an emotional rape, I remember refusing to come down to dinner on that second night. I remember hearing the door to my father's van shut, and my mother calling up to me, "Lisa, get down here. Your father's home. You're gonna piss him off if you don't come down here now." I didn't answer her.

My parents exchanged their usual pecks on the lips hello, as he entered through the back door of our kitchen, and then I heard my father ask, "Where's Lisa?"

Gently, my mother responded, "She's upstairs, babe."

"Did you call her down here?"

"Yes, but she didn't answer me. I don't know what's wrong with her," she replied to my father, once again lying, denying, invalidating -- and worse, insinuating, as if there were something inappropriate about my not wanting to be around her. At once I heard my father yell loudly and with a commanding tone, "Lisa, get your ass down here and have dinner with us – now!"

When you are eleven years old, and the adults in your life can't -- or worse, refuse to -- see what you see, how are you supposed to feel? There was no room downstairs for me. The pink elephants filled the kitchen, and I was tired of being stampeded by them. I wondered what the hell was wrong with my mother? And what the fuck was my father thinking? Why didn't he just leave me alone? Why couldn't she just tell him it was okay to let me stay in my room for a few days? Why did they have to keep pulling my skin off?

"I don't wanna come down to eat. I am not hungry," I courageously challenged my irritated father. "Get your friggin ass down here now, I said." My father's voice was slow, steady, and dripping with fire. A giant knot formed in my stomach. I would now be on display for my family. All eyes on me, the characters in my life would wait patiently for me to crack under the weight of the toxic waste that hung in the air in our kitchen. Afraid to turn my family completely inside out, I made my way down the staircase and plopped myself under the enormous pink elephant that was sitting in my seat at the table.

Mom scurried around the kitchen, quiet and on her best behavior, doing her best to perform well for my dad. It made me want to vomit, watching her avoid eye contact with me. I knew what she was doing, and she knew I knew. My father's tension was palpable. I understood the rules, however. I was to stuff what I was feeling as I was to stuff the dinner he worked hard for and she slaved over. I was to smile although I was broken, and laugh when Daddy tried to make a funny joke. I was to say "please" and "please pass the bread" and "thank you," too. I was to sit in acid and pretend not to feel a thing.

The dynamics shifted into high gear when Daddy was home. We all knew my mother didn't want to upset him, and we all knew she expected us to pretend to be happy for his sake. On this night, the knot in my stomach was so big that I wondered if it was going to project out of my mouth. She had me cornered. As with Lucey Ann, Mom expected me to make her look good in front of Dad. But if I refused to pretend and wore my emotions on my sleeve, and perhaps told my father how angry I was at his bride, she would only retreat, act taken by surprise, and point out to my father how crazy I was. The added emotional mind fuck was that I had my own individual need to make my father happy, as well.

It was all too much. The straw that broke the camel's back was when Marc pinched my thigh under the table because my leg brushed against his as I sat in my chair. Marc, sadly, enjoyed dripping acid on my wounds too. I did my best to chew my steak without letting the tears fall from my eyes. I tried to swallow, but it was impossible. The lump in my throat competed with the food in my mouth for first position in my esophagus. The muscles of my mouth found it difficult to continue chewing as my face was taken over by the emotions that had begun leaking through my cells. I remember the enormous amounts of saliva produced in my mouth. I wanted to swallow but I couldn't.

Once the vault door to the safe in my body that held my pain cracked, it was not possible for me to hold back the flood that was behind it. My body began to quiver as I did my best to sit still, and not show my father I was upset. My hands started to shake, and so I put my fork down and sat on them, so he couldn't see them tremble. I remember stretching my eye sockets to make space for the tears that were coming, in hopes that they wouldn't hit the table.

"God damn this bullshit in this friggin' house!" my father raged as he slammed his closed fist on the kitchen table. "What the frig are you crying for, huh? What -- your life around here is so friggin' bad, huh, Lisa? Your mother cooks and cleans all goddamn day; I work like a friggin' animal, so you kids can go to a nice school, and you're crying?" he yelled at me. My head was down and in my lap. We all froze. We always did when he got like that. No one moved. No one said a word.

"Get the hell outta here. Go to your room and cry. No one wants to see you cry. Get outta here; go cry in your room if you wanna cry," he said. I pushed myself away from the table and ran to my room as if I had wings. I buried myself deep under my blankets, and stuffed my mouth into a pillow, and cried cries I could not hold back. Like wild horses, the tears and the aching broke free.

I could hear my father raging and ranting down in the kitchen. I stuffed my fingers in my ears in an attempt not to hear what he was saying, but he was so loud, and our house was so small, I heard every word. “It’s okay, Ross -- relax. I told you she was like this, Ross. I don’t know what we’re going to do with her. Ignore her, Ross. Come on, I made you a wonderful dinner, don’t let her ruin it. Come on, kids, let’s eat.” Slowly, my father’s voice began to wane, and the chaotic balance in the home was once again achieved. Everything was back to normal. Mommy had appeased Daddy. Marc and Leslie were smiling at the dinner table, slipping under the rug too. I, the most raw of the bunch, was up in my room, alone, doing my best not to slip between the cracks that blanketed my mind.

The Games I Learned to Play

1,2, 3, 4, 5, 6, 7, 8, 9, 10. I liked even numbers. Soon after I broke up with my pen, the counting started. In my head, I began counting the letters to the sentences I overheard people speak. I would visualize the letters in my mind, and then count each letter, anticipating it landing on a 10. A sentence like "She ran fast" was perfect, because the letters in the sentence totaled 10. A sentence like "It's really cold outside" was also perfect, because when I'd count the letters in that sentence on my fingers, the sentence ended on 20. If a sentence didn't end on a 10, a 20, or a 30, in my mind I would add letters to a word until it did.

No one knew I was counting. No one knew that while conversations were being had, I was matching my fingers to the letters in their sentences. I would hold my hands behind my back, stiffen my thumb, and tap each other finger against my thumb, starting with my pinky, until in my mind, I contorted a sentence till it landed on a ten.

I counted all the time. It soothed me. And although it may sound bizarre and even whacky to most, the truth is it wasn't as insane as it sounds. As a child, I had nowhere to turn with my feelings. Assault after assault only added more pain to my already tender body. No one saw me. No one valued me as a feeling being, despite the immense feelings in my being. In one unspoken message I was being told not to feel, and to never express how I feel, while in the next I was being shown that only Mommy and Daddy had the right to feel as well as to express their emotions. My world was a topsy-turvy one, which left me dazed with inconsistencies, and a feeling of distrust for those I had no other choice but to call my family.

Counting was also my way of staying inside my head and away from my mother. I had found a way to do something she couldn't control. And as abnormal as this behavior seemed, in my heart I believe it saved me from being taken over by the tornado of guilt and shame that had become my constant companions. I secretly counted in my mind from the moment I woke up in the morning until the moment I fell asleep. When there weren't any conversations going on around me, I would make one up in my head, and feel almost accomplished, validated, or worthy when I was able to come up with a sentence that neatly landed on a ten. My mother couldn't invalidate what she didn't know existed.

Aside from counting letters, I also developed an obsession with license plates. On my way to school in the morning, I would memorize plate numbers and repeat them over and over in my mind, and see how long I could remember the number, until I saw another plate number I liked. During the Sunday morning drives to my grandparents' house in Maspeth, and while both my parents filled the car with their cigarette smoke, I would float away by focusing on all the plate numbers that were passing us by on the streets. When I was lost in the land of numbers, I was less conscious and tuned into what my mother, father, or brother might have been thinking of me. Caring more about the numbers that danced in my head helped me care less about what anyone I cared about thought about me.

I loved to write. I wrote poems, and short stories. Once I even wrote a script for the show *The Hardy Boys.* I was deeply infatuated with Sean Cassidy. Its plot centered around a little girl who was sick, who of course would have been played by me. While I cannot recall the entire basis of the story line, I do remember dreaming about Sean Cassidy and Parker Stevenson coming to my emotional rescue. I was so convinced the story was TV-worthy that I sent it to the show's producer, who I think was Glen Larson. I acquired his address through a teen magazine.

Hair pulling also soothed me. It was a habit I developed one afternoon while I sat on my bed. My mother and I had just had one of our blow-outs. I remember feeling particularly cut that afternoon, because on that day, while in the throes of her rage she called me a "psycho" and said I was going to be "just like Aunt Evelyn." I can't even remember what I did that day. Much of the time, Mom expected me to read her mind, and know she wanted me to bring the shoes that were on the staircase up to the bedrooms. Sometimes she went off into a tirade after Daddy gave her a hard time on the phone. Sometimes she just got so worked up over all the laundry, that just my sitting on the couch pissed her off. It was easier for me to just get up and leave, or stay in my room.

Often Mom would not stop beating me up with her words until she was able to break me. I realized that when I finally cracked, and started to double over and cry, then she'd stop screaming at me. It was amazing, really. It was as if she were in a boxing ring with me, and her words were her fist and I was her opponent, and the fight went on until she was able to knock me out. My tears and grimacing expressions, or when I'd finally be pushed to punch a wall or make a fist, were the signs of the knockout. All at once, her defensive words would cease, the anger in her voice would drift off, and an expression almost of accomplishment would wash over her face.

Terrified I'd end up like Aunt Evelyn, and unsure I wasn't going to, I hushed the visions of myself in a straitjacket out of my head by focusing instead on isolating single strands of hair with my fingers. "No, no, no ... I am not like Aunt Evelyn. No, no, no ... I am not crazy ... no, no, no ... it's okay to dream about Sean Cassidy. I know it's only a show.... No, no, no..." I remember repeating these phrases as I twirled hair around my fingers, and then yanked hard, eased by the welcome relief summoned by the sting of pulling hair out of my head. The pricking to my scalp made sense. This pain I could account for. My mother's rage, however, was never something I could quite comprehend, except when, in my mind, I innocently accepted responsibility for it.

Outside, focused on my physical reality, was too bitter for me to tolerate for long periods of time. Counting letters to sentences, obsessively recalling license plates, fantasizing about whimsical ideas about love, and hair pulling kept whatever piece of mind that had not been singed by the incomprehensible exposure to the chill of emotionally abusive frostbite from falling off the cliff of my psyche. Without my pen, the garbage was piling up. These obsessions helped me deal with the rot.

Sore Thumb

Low self-worth isn't like a cold. It's not something you get over in ten days. When you do not possess any sense of value for your self, it shows. Children are masterfully intuitive, especially when it comes to other children. They know intrinsically which children amongst them can be bullied and which children cannot. Bullied children don't wear signs around their necks asking to get bullied. But they do give off signs that indicate to others that they do not feel like they belong. Their cues lie in their physicality. Their posture is usually droopy, clumsy, or stiff. They rarely have the desire or the strength to look someone else in the eyes. They either avoid getting physically close to others, or sometimes they are overly clingy. While it might be difficult for an adult to pick out from a crowd the children who are most likely to suffer from bullying in their lifetime, a child, on the other hand, could single them out with ease.

I wasn't the typical bullied child, however. From the outside looking in, my posture didn't droop, and my body wasn't particularly stiff. I know this, because I can specifically remember consciously telling myself not to droop or to walk like a board. In my mind, I was aware I wasn't like everyone else, and my aim was to pretend like I didn't care.

I suppose looking back, at school, I very much put myself in the position of the observer of my experience, as opposed to truly absorbing the abuse like I did at home. By the time I was ten or eleven, my relationship with my mother had pretty much secured my distrust in others. The tough skin being a member of my family required served me well, or so I presumed. I could never have known then how the armor I believed protected me was in reality more like a matador's red cape.

While I was terribly bullied at school, as well as at home, the dynamics in me were not the same. The lack of empathy my mother had for me as her child pierced me far more deeply than the rejection I received at school. Believing I was unloved and ultimately rejected by my own mother was all but fatal to my soul. While I wished I had fit in at school, the fact of not fitting in didn't incapacitate me, like one might think it could have. I believe my ability to see myself apart from the children at school served me well in regard to bullying. I went in, knowing I wasn't like them. I went in shielded. I went in not trusting.

I always felt that I confused the other kids in my class. While we all knew I was different, I didn't cower like some of the other bullied kids did. If a bully made fun of me, I made fun of him back. If a bully hit me, I struck him back, but twice as hard. And if a group of kids ganged up on me in the schoolyard, I waited them out, until one day I found them alone and punished them then. I may not have been dainty or little, like most girls my age, but I was strong, and I wasn't afraid to use my physical strength in my defense.

The boys picked on me far more than the girls did. I think the girls knew I'd kick their asses if they went too far. Aside from two ratty-looking girls named Carlene and Monique, I never had any real issues with girls. The boys were my problem.

I wasn't a boy, but I wasn't a girl -- at least not to the boys in my class, anyway. Uncertain how to treat me, they were confused by the "thing" that I was. My bullies called me names like "The Man," "The Chimp," "The Thing," "The He/She," and "Herc." They poked fun at my hairy arms and the mop on my head. They enjoyed tripping me as I walked down an aisle, and especially thought spitting on my seat or wiping snot on my pencils was funny.

I hated Wednesdays. We had gym class on Wednesdays, which meant I was going to be punished physically for being who I was, or for who I wasn't. Our gym teacher insisted we play dodge ball. I often wondered why we just couldn't do laps around the gym, or do sit-ups, or jumping jacks instead. How could it have been that our teacher did not see what went on during our recreational period?

My only defense was to try to avoid getting hit. The captains rarely picked me to be on their teams because history had revealed that I was the most popular target in the class. If you were on my team, and if by chance you were standing next to me when the other team had the ball, there was a good possibility you were going to get reamed hard if the other team missed me, their true target.

I can still feel the sting of the dodge ball against my bare legs, and the sound I heard inside my head whenever the tough ball slammed into my skull. The expressions on the boys' faces frightened me. I hated knowing that not only did they enjoy getting me out of the game, but more disturbing was the fact that they reveled in hurting me in the process. This wasn't a form of wholesome fun. To the contrary, this game was a form of supervised bullying.

Timothy was a fat, red-haired, freckle-faced kid in our class who had been left back. He hated me, and he made it known. For whatever the reason, the boys in my class were afraid of him. The bullies gladly gave up their reigns to the big-mouthed fat kid the minute he walked into our homeroom. Timothy was your typical smartass-type kid, who wasn't intimidated by authority. He was the only kid I ever saw in my whole eight years in Catholic school who ever had the audacity to make fun of a nun behind her back. I was taken aback that he didn't even care what God might think.

I hated him too. And I let him know it in my own way. I didn't laugh when he spit spit balls at the back of our teachers' skirts, nor did I give him the attention he craved when he acted dumb when he was called on to ask a question. I refused to gather around him when he told dirty jokes in the schoolyard, and when he bragged about taking uppers and downers, I made sure to appear disinterested.

Whenever we went to any other part of our school building, we were expected to get there in rows. The rows were divided into two. One line was for the boys and the other was for the girls. Timothy was tall, since he was a year older, so his spot was in the back of the boys' line. We also traveled in size order. I was tall for a girl, and stood toward the back of the girls' line. One morning, as our class made its way down to the first floor, Timothy, behind Sister Rose Georgette's back, took up a fighting stance beside me as if he were preparing to box me. The boys in front of Timothy all laughed. My gut told me he was going to take a swing at me, and expected me to be quiet about it, because he assumed I feared him like the rest of the cowards in my class did. But Timothy didn't know that this he/she hit back.

Timothy bobbed and weaved for a few steps, and made many of the boys laugh. Once or twice, Sister Rose Georgette stopped to take a peek at what was going on in the back of the line. She had heard some snickering, but was unable to catch Timothy in his boxing act. I continued to stare forward, but kept one eye on Timothy the whole time. As Sister Rose Georgette began to take up her walk again, and as our lines followed, Timothy punched me in the left arm with all his might. Having been semi- prepared for the punch, I stiffened my shoulder muscle, braced my body and absorbed the blow as best I could. Without hesitating, I cocked my right arm back, clenched my fist, and with all my might, and just like my father had taught me to do since I was a little girl, I punched Timothy dead square in the center of his shoulder, with all my body weight behind the force.

I hated fighting, but I hated anyone thinking they were going to push me around and get away with it even more. Being bullied in school was sort of like being bullied at home. I sort of had to take it, most of the time. But unlike Mom, I could hit a bully back, if they hit me. Of course, fighting back only made the dodge ball beatings, the name-calling, the snotty pencils, and the accidental tripping worse, but the glory that came on the days I actually got to strike back helped to even the score -- at least a little.

Who, Me?

I cringed when the teacher made the announcement. For the upcoming science fair, we would have to pair off with a partner. I didn't want a partner. Or perhaps, I was all too aware that there probably wasn't anyone in my class who wanted me as a partner anyway. The teacher paired me up with a wavy- haired girl named Janice. She was quiet and non-intimidating. She was the type of girl who ran away from the dodge ball when it came her direction, and let out an "Aaaah" when it came too close. Although her hair was frizzy, it was long, and she had the most exquisite-colored eyes. They reminded me of marcasite.

Janice and I decided to do a report on the circulatory system. We met at the local library a few days after school to gather information. Back then we had to rely on good old encyclopedias and bulky Xerox machines. I was surprised at how easily Janice let me take the lead. I liked science and was always captivated by the synchronicity of the human body. If it hadn't been mandatory to work with a partner on this project, I knew I would have gotten an A. Despite what was going on at home and at school, I was an achiever.

Once we gathered enough information, it was time to pull our work together in an impressive presentation. Janice said it was okay with her mom for us to do the rest of the work at their home. Their home was disorganized. It didn't look like mine. My mother and father were meticulous about fingerprints on doorjambs, and pieces of lint on the rugs. My mother was a scrubber and professional organizer, and my father was a handyman and an organizer. Janice's house didn't seem like any scrubbers, handymen, or organizers lived there.

The house was filled with people. She lived with her one older sister and two younger sisters, as well as two of her cousins, and her mom and dad. It seemed as if every time I looked up, another body was walking through the kitchen, where we had all our materials spread out across the family's eating table. What impressed me the most was how nice they all seemed to be toward one another, and how warmly they greeted me.

It didn't take long for me to fall in love with the feelings I found in Janice's house. I remember tossing and turning inside my mind. I told myself to stop wanting my friendship with her to last once the project had been handed in. I struggled to remind myself of the fact that Janice and I had met only because the teacher insisted we work on our projects together. Janice didn't like me, I scolded myself. She had to deal with me. She had no other choice. And besides, her life was so full of wonderful other relationships, why on earth would she want an outcast like me hanging out with her?

I had found contentment in the spanking I had done to my mind for wanting my friendship with Janice to continue once the project had been turned in. And on that day, when Janice and I presented our work to the teacher, I was prepared for my life to return back to its tawdry norm. It was what it was, I thought, and I wasn't about to stick my neck out so she could step on it.

I was just about to cross 15th Avenue on my way home that same day when I heard someone say, "Wanna come hang out with me and my sisters today?" It was Janice. Confused, and teetering on the brink of terror as well as of joyful possibility, I was unsure of how to answer. The truth was, I wasn't sure if I wanted to go. I was sure, however, that I didn't want to get hurt. I was sure I liked how I felt when I was around her and her family. But I wasn't sure I could let her or those good feelings in. And I wasn't sure I would be strong enough to handle being rejected by her if I were somehow able to learn to let my guard down.

"Sure," I said, "but I have to call my mom to tell her where I am, when we get to your house."

Can I Trust You?

As we walked to Janice's house, I tried not to get too caught up in the tug of war that was happening in my mind. There was a part of me that could not comprehend why Janice wanted to hang out with me. Our project had already been turned in. My mind could not make sense of her extending herself to someone like me. But there was also another part of me who felt compelled to take the risk.

Apprehension began to soften as Janice and I made our way to her home that afternoon. I called Mom and let her know where I was. She was fine with my hanging out with Janice, and just asked that I be home for dinner. Janice's bedroom was tight, and she shared her room with her sisters. There were clothes strewn about, and I remember being taken back by the underwear and bras that were so aimlessly tossed upon the floor, so without regard for modesty. I liked that Janice and her family were not phased by such things. It helped ease my raw skin.

Unsteady on my feet while in such close emotional proximity to others, I remember trying not to appear anxious at their openness toward one another. I found myself more passively observing and absorbing than interacting. I didn't know how to act. I didn't know what was appropriate. So accustomed to living my life waiting for the fatal blow to strike, I found it emotionally straining to sit on the edge of their bunk bed, amongst dirty articles of clothing, listening to the silly, open laughter that was going on among Janice, her sisters, and her cousin Nancy. I kept waiting to be attacked for something -- my hair, my teeth, my eyebrows, something. But the assault never came. That was odd.

Much to my surprise, my friendship with Janice continued. I found myself feeling less alone, and as if this family of sisters had sucked me in. Janice, her sisters, and their cousins were close. And when I came along, I was simply accepted as one of them. It was hard not to drop my guard, but it was even harder for me not to gravitate toward the newness that was sweeping me up. It was as if this one friendship changed my whole world, or at least my perception of it.

Janice and I were friends at school. too. Ordinarily I ate lunch alone. But since our science project, Janice and I were now sharing lunch periods. The bullies were less irritating now, or perhaps because I felt less like a sore thumb, I wasn't as preoccupied with being on guard. Things were turning around. Even Mom treated me better. I felt that maybe she was happy I had found a friend.

As time went on, Janice and I began sharing secrets, like little girls do. Both infatuated with boys, we'd talk for hours about how cute this or that boy was. It felt incredibly freeing to open up and laugh with her the way I learned to do. I had gained trust in her as well as in myself, and in my thoughts, enough to share what was on my mind. Janice was as silly as I was. I had no reason not to trust my new friend.

I eventually opened up to her and told her about the mad crush I had on a boy in one of the other seventh-grade homerooms. His name was Scott. Scott was tall, had hair the color of sand, and eyes that reminded me of a Caribbean sea. He was a thin boy, with large white teeth that seemed too big for his mouth. But I didn't care. What I really liked about Scott was that although I had never actually spoken to him, I could not help but notice that he was quieter than the other obnoxious boys in our collective seventh-grade class.

Scott didn't know it, but I watched him from afar. During the morning line-ups, I would keep a watchful eye on him. Never once did I witness him tease a girl, or push another boy around. His demeanor was strong, and appeared confident. When he spoke to his friends, he looked them in the eye, and always seemed to be smiling at them, as if he were drawing them into him. He gave me the impression that he was easy to like, and that he liked others easily. This, of course, was all in my mind.

Janice was a good listener. She encouraged me to continue liking Scott. She told me she was sure he would like me if he knew I liked him, and that perhaps one day, she and I would get the courage to tell him. I appreciated her kind words, but I was well aware that my sentiments for Scott would have to stay in my mind. I was cognizant of what I looked like, and I knew that Scott was out of my league. A boy like him could never like a girl like me. Dreaming about him, and endlessly chatting the afternoons away with Janice about him, were purely for entertainment purposes only. That was enough for me.

Janice had a secret, too, except it had nothing to do with boys. One afternoon, a few weeks into our friendship, she asked me to walk her to the boulevard. She said she wanted to go into the Woolworth's store. After school, we walked to the store together. I followed behind Janice. When we got to the make-up aisle, Janice stopped, turned to look at me, and then slid a lip pencil up her coat sleeve. My eyes grew wide, and my heart thumped loudly as my brain tried to make sense of what was going on.

Janice put her finger to her lips as if to tell me to shush. My body stiffened; I suddenly felt as if the entire world were watching us now. Janice made her way up and down a few more aisles, with me following closely in tow. Uncertain of how to act, I kept quiet and followed her lead out the door. My mind raced as I tried to come to terms with what she had done. I was taken aback by her cleverness, and relaxed sense of being. I would have expected her to be shaken, anxious, or perhaps even frightened. But there was none of that in her. In fact, Janice seemed downright giddy, and even proud.

Janice led me straight to her bedroom when we got to her house. Once there, she opened up her pockets, and pulled out an array of stolen items from Woolworth's. Pencils, erasers, and lip glosses toppled out of her jacket like popcorn pops out of a machine. I was dazed by the number of items she had stolen under my nose without my noticing.

I walked to my house that night with a heavy heart. Our class was to make the Sacrament of Confirmation that year. I wondered if Janice ever paid attention to what Mrs. Agnello was teaching us in religion about the Holy Spirit, and the Sacrament of Confirmation. Didn't she know that stealing was wrong? Didn't she know how sad she was making Jesus by stealing? Didn't she hear what the teacher said about Confirmation? Mrs. Agnello explained that we, as young Christians, were now going to be responsible for our spiritual walk with Christ. Didn't Janice know that God was watching her, and me?

I had been struck by what Mrs. Agnello had been teaching, and although I despised the tremendous sculpture of a bloodied Jesus Christ that hung over our church's altar, I believed I loved Jesus. I did not want to disappoint the man, or the God, who came to this earth to save my soul. I was not clear about all the specific details, but I was convinced there was a God. And I was even more convinced He knew His way to Woolworth's, too.

The next day at school, Janice asked me to walk her to the Woolworth's store after our last class. I came up with a bogus excuse, and passed on the invitation. I found myself in a familiar battle zone. My mind tugged from side to side, and struggled with feelings of disappointment, sadness, fear, intimidation, and especially guilt. Janice was my friend. She was my only friend, and now nothing felt the same. It was impossible for me to fake it. At lunch, I was more reserved than usual, and Janice noticed. In fact she called me out on it. "What's up your ass?" I remember her asking.

I didn't feel comfortable telling her my secrets anymore. I was pulling back. The guilt I felt about Janice's secret was overwhelming. Nothing felt the same anymore. "You're coming with me today to Woolworth's," she demanded. I agreed to tag along, but in my mind I had already decided that I would not go inside the store with her. I kept that fact to myself, and shuddered quietly in my shoes.

I hoped it would pass. The guilt in me covered me like a lead suit. It never left me. I hoped Janice would respect my feelings about her secret. I hoped she would understand how uncomfortable stealing made me feel. I hoped I wouldn't lose the only friend I had over this, but I wasn't sure I wouldn't. I decided to play the game out, and to see what would happen next.

"There is a green notebook I want in there. It has a puppy on the cover. Go in there and steal it for me," Janice demanded, as we stood outside the Woolworth's store on a chilly afternoon. Her face turned to ice when I said, "No, I can't do that for you. If you want it, then you go. I am too afraid of getting caught."

"Go in there and get me that notebook, or I won't be your friend anymore, Lisa," she barked back through clenched teeth. The fatal blow crept up on me, like a sucker punch, and almost knocked me down for the count right there on the cold pavement below my feet.

I stood there for a moment and looked down at Janice. She was shorter than I. I felt as if my life were passing in front of my eyes. All my hopes, all the newness, disintegrated in a flash. My trust in Janice had been lost. She was just like everyone else, I thought. She cared only about herself, and she never really saw me at all. I didn't want to believe it, but I really had been only a science project partner. I was never really one of her sisters, or even her cousin. I was just some other character in her life whom she thought she could manipulate into doing for her what she wanted others to do. She knew how lonely I had been, and how bullied I was. I told her. I had trusted her with all of that, and here she was, using my wound as a weapon against me. Now I was sorry I had ever met her.

Mrs. Agnello had said that being a good Christian would mean having to take a stand for what we believed was right. She said that the Ten Commandments were like a guideline for people to pay attention to. She said that God was always present, even when we were tempted to do wrong, and that He would give us the strength when we needed it to do what was right. She said that the uncomfortable feelings we get in our bellies were actually the Holy Spirit's way of talking to us. She said that when we felt bad, that was a signal from our higher power that we were going against what was right and good. She said that if we didn't listen to our gut, it was akin to laughing at Christ while He hung on the cross. Christ came to help save our souls from temptation. Giving into evil was the equivalent to spitting in the face of our Savior.

"I swear to God, Lisa, if you don't go in and get me that notebook, I will never speak to you again," she reiterated, as my gut made up my mind. I turned away from Janice, and never looked back. And as I took what seemed like the longest walk home, I mentally began sloughing her out of my being. She wasn't who I had hoped she was. We weren't who I hoped we were. And tomorrow would certainly be hell. It was an amazing moment in my life. Looking back at that walk home now, as the observer of the child I was, I cannot help but feel proud of my decision to walk away from Janice that day. What she could never have known was that although I didn't like being friendless, I hated being pushed around even more.

On that long walk home, I heard for the first time a voice I had never known. It was hardly audible, and it sounded more like whimpering than it did a conversation. But deep down inside me somewhere, I sensed I had connected to something profound. I had the faint idea that it was highly improbable that I was all bad, like I had always believed.

Janice held to her word. She never spoke to me again. It was as if we had never shared that science project. It was as if I'd never met her sisters or her cousins, and we'd never shoplifted at Woolworth's. In one swift decision, my whole life turned back on its thorny side again, only this time it was by my choice. I was beginning to understand that in order to survive this world, I would need to regress further into my own.

The Tipping Point

It was the first day of eighth grade. My sentence at this hell of a Catholic school would be over in approximately nine months. Like every other first day back to school after a long summer, each of the grades were expected to line up in their assigned spots in the schoolyard. Back then our school was overcrowded. Each grade had at least three homerooms. My assigned line stood between each of the other eighth-grade homeroom classes.

The schoolyard was buzzing with children, and parents lined the silver chain link fence that surrounded the perimeter of the enclosed area in which the grades stood. Right before the principal clanged the large bronze bell that sounded the "quiet" signal, a ruckus began to emerge in the street outside the yard. One by one, children from the eighth-grade lines started darting outside the gate to gather in the street. From where I stood inside the yard, it looked like the crowd was encircling someone. However, I was unable to make out who was getting all the attention, and could not imagine why anyone would be, so early in the morning, and in the year.

The bell rang, and like trained puppies, the children neatly dispensed themselves to their proper places on their respective class lines. As the crowd thinned, I was taken back by what had been the cause of the stir. The diluted horde revealed my worst and unimagined nightmare. Like a celebrity couple fending off a drove of adoring fans, Janice and Scott appeared hand in hand.

Nothing I had ever been through before could have prepared me for the rush of vile adrenaline that gushed through my thin veins. I could neither fight nor flee. I felt gutted, and as if my intestines were lying on the ground at my feet. Worse, I was dying, and no one around me knew how close to death I was. Similar to the rawness I felt when under attack by my mother's rage, but far more intense than any other murdering emotion I had experienced, seeing Janice and Scott together made me feel like death had come instantly. There was no room to flee to, no pen to flow with, no place to pull my hair, no words to count, or license plates to fall in love with. This tsunami of acid, I would have to swim in.

As an older soul these days, as well as a mother of three, I have many times reflected on how it is or why it is some children are so cold-hearted and cruel to other children. It boggles my adult mind to consider the notion that there are children who delight in the act of inflicting emotional and psychological violence on other children. It is beyond the edges of my mind to fully grasp the insensitive nature one must possess in order to look forward to destroying another human being, especially when the persecutors and the victims are children. On that fateful morning, as Janice gave me a contented vengeful look, as she made her way to the back of the line, I sank into the vat of poison that had become the familiar lightless theme of my life. There was no room left for "whys" now.

Darkness had begun to touch the edges of my mind, like morning fog hugs the shore. This wasn't as simple as it seemed -- at least not to me, and certainly not for Janice. It was deeper than my old friend now dating the guy I had a crush on. It was danker than jealousy. In fact, there was not a hint of jealousy in me. All I could feel was enormous grief. Like a swarm of wasps, emotions ricocheted inside my being, repeatedly stinging me from the inside out. I wasn't angry or envious. I oozed despair over the depths of Janice's disregard for the trust I bestowed on her, and for the depths of her desire to retaliate against me for my simply not wanting to do what she wanted me to do. It was a vengeful act I could not wrap my psychological fingers around.

To add further insult to my already bleeding injuries, the summer had transformed Janice from a dull wallflower into a stunning bird of paradise. To say that this young girl was beautiful would be to underemphasize the truth of her newfound beauty. Janice no longer wore a mane of wool. Her eyebrows no longer mimicked furry pretzels. And her eyes no longer turned downward when others looked into them. Time, infused with just the right amount of female hormones, had morphed Janice into what could have been described only as a twelve-year-old bombshell. She resembled nothing of the Janice I knew who liked to steal from the local variety store. This girl I didn't know. This girl scared me. This girl held my soul in her hand, and we both knew it. I could only hope she didn't squeeze it too hard.

It was difficult to get my legs to move. The walk to the third floor felt incredibly longer than usual. I was holding myself together by threads. Scott wasn't in our homeroom. I was thankful that at least I didn't have to witness them sharing glances or exchanging notes back and forth. As I struggled to accept this new reality, simultaneously, all at once, my hankering to daydream about Scott perished. The yearning was gone. One more secret escape of mine, exposed.

It is hard to conceive that no one knew how close to the brink I was, especially Janice. She didn't stop finding ways to let me know her dating Scott was more than what it seemed. There was a motive behind her actions, although there was no one I could have shared that with besides her, and certainly no one who cared, or would believe me, either. Janice made sure to walk by my desk more times than necessary, and each time she did, she either bumped into my leg, or pretended to trip so she could fall on top of me. Once or twice I dared to look over my shoulder at her, only to discover her speckled gray eyes staring back at me, as she dangled between her fingers the ankle bracelet Scott gave her.

Out of my league, I surrendered. This was not a fight I was going to win. This war wasn't about physical strength or agility. This was a war that raged on a delicate and fragile landscape. Janice was much stronger than I emotionally. She had a support system I didn't, and now she even had Scott. I wished she'd try to beat me up at the park, or had pulled my hair during gym. If she had tried to hurt me physically, I was sure I could have hurt her back, and even more than she ever could have hurt me. This war had not only taken me by surprise, but it was also taking place in a part of my soul that was already paper-thin.

Punctured by her betrayal, and even more by her need to rub my blood in my face, I could feel myself slipping, as if life were being drained out of me. I hoped the day would end quickly, in spite of the way time felt like it had stopped. But sadly the day only got worse, as time proved even more suffering was on its way.

"Champion, you're disgusting. You're the ugliest fucking thing I have ever seen in my life. You make me sick. I don't want you thinking about me, writing poems about me, or even fucking talking about me. You are so ugly; you look like a fucking guy. You're so ugly, you're probably a fucking lesbian. You fucking bitch. Don't ever even look at me, you fucking ugly cunt," Scott said, as he stood in the doorway of my classroom during our lunch period, with my old and only friend I ever had by his side … Janice.

The Message

If it is possible to survive a psychological mutilation, then survive it is what I did, at least momentarily anyway. I am forty-six years old, and I can still find within me, resonating however deeply, the pangs inflicted against my soul that day. I weep now as an observer for the innocent child I once was. I was guilty only of wanting a friend in whom I could trust with a little part of me, and Janice not only punished me by withdrawing from me, but unzipped my soul, yanked out whatever sliver was left, and tap-danced on it with razor-sharp heels. And although I am much, much wiser today than then, I still find myself encumbered by the inability to comprehend reasons for such disregard, insensitivity, and emotional torture.

I remember going deaf as my head turned toward the doorway where Scott and Janice stood. I remember my veins growing cold, and feeling as if my toes and fingers were sitting in ice. My head got heavy, and my vision began to fade. My heart pounded in my chest, and for a second I wondered if it were going to land in my lap. As the other children in my class began to chuckle at my expense, I began to feel as if I were evaporating right there at my desk.

Scott would have gone on with his attack had it not been for Janice tugging on his arm. An idea came to me almost immediately after they left the doorway. When I got home, I was going to end my life. The suffering in me had reached a critical point. There were no more places for me to hide. There were no more numbers I could count. And there were no more dreams I felt safe enough to dream. Death would save me, I thought, from the wretchedness of being punished for being who I was, whoever I was. I could not face Scott or Janice another day. There was nothing left in me that I could grasp onto, which might save me from the fire that had consumed my life.

As if I were floating on a cloud, ideas of death helped guide me home. I knew where it was. Daddy had shown me how to shoot it. He told me that if anyone ever broke into our house, that I was to shoot them dead, and not worry about it. He showed me the place where he kept it. It was tucked on his side of the bed, between the mattress and the box spring. He said it wasn't a toy.

It was heavier than I had thought it would be. As Mom vacuumed one of the rooms beneath her bedroom where I stood with the gun pressed against the side of my head, I wondered if she'd hear the gun go off over the rumbling of the vacuum cleaner. I pictured my brains and my blood dripping down her walls, and wondered if she'd cry when she found my lifeless body. I wasn't afraid, as vision after vision popped into my mind's eye. I saw myself dead, in a white casket, my classmates surrounding my body. I imagined Janice and Scott feeling guilty for being so cruel.

It was cold. The barrel of the gun hurt the right side of my head. I was pressing the gun firmly against my temple. The visions had taken over my ability to see. Blinded by the sweet scent of relief, I had lost any understanding of the reality of where my thoughts had led. My hand began to shake when I turned to peek at myself in the mirror that hung in my mother's bedroom. Reality stared back at me; my sight returned, kicking and screaming, clawing to gain first place over the intoxicating imagined visions in my brain.

As stark reality emerged, layers of emotions began to crumble. Unexpected tears found their ways to the portholes of my soul, and soon flooded. It was impossible to keep the gun pressed against my head; my hands trembling, I placed the gun down on the dresser below the mirror. My body began to heave loads of thick emotions out of me, almost vomiting them up, as standing still became almost impossible.

For the first time in my life, I saw … me. The vision of myself, with a gun pressed against the side of my head, with waves of tears flowing out of me like a river, startled my mind into awakening. A reactive participant to the pain that had been my life, so consumed by my attempts to survive emptiness, I had failed to recognize my pain as an observer. Being void of this outer perspective had kept me trapped inside a cycle of never-ending torture. This reflection, although terrifying, allowed me to "see" my feelings. For the first time, I felt a hint of validation. Because no one I ever cared for had reflected a sense of worth back to me, I was cheated out of the ability to "see me" and to value my feelings, all my life long.

Ideas of death were quickly replaced with concerns of consequence. An inkling of perspective allowed my mind to place space between my insurmountable pain, and death. I came to understand that it was not death that I wanted. What I truly craved was relief. I wanted the pain to stop, even for just a day. I wanted to go to school and not be bullied. I wanted to walk past Mom and not feel like who I was disgusted her. I wanted to wake up and not feel like what I looked like mattered so much. I didn't want to have to pretend for Daddy that I was happy if I weren't. For one day, I just wanted to feel free, and maybe even secure in my own skin.

With perspective came more tears. Like a floodgate door had suddenly been opened, and as if my heart were throwing up, sheets of disappointments came unraveled. The greater emotional distance I gained from my own self's pain, the deeper were the cries of my soul. As if experiencing my pain through an outer body awareness, with eyes that were not my own, "me" -- who "I" was -- became more real than ever before. I could no longer pretend not to feel. I could see "me" now, and that included some of what I had forgotten.

Exasperated, I fell crippled to the shaking in my body. Rattled by the emulsion of toxic emotions, I struggled to stay on my feet. I could not think my thoughts. They happened upon me on their own. Thought after thought entered my mind, like gnats. It was impossible for me to focus. As my body stood shaking, and as tears flowed freely, I heard a voice crack the silence in my mother's bedroom. The voice was clear. I was certain I heard it. It was commanding but non-threatening, and this is what it said: "Lisa, put down the gun. One day you will show them."

I wondered if I were crazy. I wondered if my mother were right. Maybe I was like Aunt Evelyn after all. I feared the voice was not real. I tried not to draw parallels between the voice and Starsky and Hutch. I tried to tell myself I hadn't heard a voice at all, but inside me I could not escape this sense that I had heard what I'd heard. The voice was neither female or male. The voice did not frighten me, and in fact, I found comfort in its arrival.

Back from the brink of suicide, I slowly began to reintegrate. My mind would need to reorganize its thoughts, if my life were to go on. As I slumped into exhaustion, my back slid down the bedroom wall, and I sank to my knees. Crawling on all fours, I neatly slipped the gun back into its resting place, and then rolled up into a ball on the rug next to my father's side of the bed. I could not stay there for very long. My uniform was beginning to wrinkle, and if Mom found me there, she would not be pleased.

My Brothers Guardian

I went to bed extra early that night. The day had stolen far too many breaths from me. Sleep would take me away, I hoped, and help me vacation, at least for a while, from the Ferris Wheel of life. Many decisions had been made that afternoon. Above all, I had decided that suicide could never be a valid option for escaping the harrows of my existence. Instead, I had concluded that pain was most definitely going to be a part of my life. I would never escape. Pain was inevitable for a person like me, I thought.

I came to conclusions about my "self," as well. Amidst the avalanche of tears, and the volcano of erupting emotions, I found ideas I had never unearthed before. Beneath it all, and perhaps as the result of the erupting of the layers of negative emotions, I discovered a truth about myself I had never known. The idea that I was unworthy began to thin as I came into the awareness that much of why I did not kill myself that day had to do with my worrying about what the consequences of my suicide would be to my family. Although the pain in me was severe, I made a conscious decision not to commit suicide because of what my family would have to endure once I was gone.

As reality brought in ideas of consequence, I pondered that day, as I looked into the mirror, what my sister, brother, mother, and father would have to go through as a result of my suicide. I imagined my little sister being pointed at, and Marc being made fun of because his sister was "crazy." I saw vividly Marc and Leslie being teased because of what I had done, and felt strongly in my gut the frustration I would feel if I were watching from afar, and unable to protect them from the ill thoughts of others. I imagined my mother holding my corpse in her arms, with a gaping hole in my head, weeping hysterically at the sight of her dead daughter. I imagined how my father might feel, losing both his daughter and mother to suicide.

Lying in bed that night, I found myself feeling almost proud for not pulling the trigger that afternoon. In not pulling the trigger, I discovered a sense of self-worth. It was love that kept that bullet in that gun and out of my head. In realizing that I did not kill myself because I wanted to spare my family any anguish as a backlash for my suicide, I found a hint of self-worth. I recognized that it had to be impossible for me "not to be good." I had to be worthy. I wasn't selfish, and I wasn't crazy, either. I loved my family enough to endure whatever whirlwind was coming my direction in the following days, and I decided that holding on in the face of it was indeed my purpose. In notions like these, I found the courage to face the days ahead, in spite of the days that had come and gone.

My family would never know the sacrifice I had made for their sake. I could never share with them what was going on at school, or the fact that I was so unhappy I wanted to die. I kept what was happening at school a secret, afraid my mother would only blame me -- or worse, find my ideas of suicide reason to have me committed to a mental institution. After Scott slaughtered me that day in the classroom, I retreated further into myself. I grew more irritable and self-protective. I spent even less time with my family, and found refuge in long rides on my bike. They could never have known that in all my fleeing was the love I felt so deeply for them all. I fled to spare them being irritated by the sight of me, and also as a way to detach myself from the bitterness created by the need to flee.

I could see why Marc despised me. Never very good at schoolwork, Marc was often compared to me by my parents, but especially by my father. "Goddamn it, Marc. Look at Lisa's work. Why can't you write like she writes? If she can do it, you can do it. You're friggin' lazy. That's your problem. You're a goddamn dumbass," my father would shout, at Marc, while Leslie and I sat at our desks after school, trying to do homework. Nothing Marc ever did was quite enough for my father. I always felt sad for Marc, and wished sincerely that he wouldn't blame me for how my father compared the two of us. In my heart, I could feel his pain, but my eyes told me he hated me.

I'd learned to grow a thicker skin that year in eighth grade. No one could hurt me now. I no longer cared to make friends, or wondered what Janice or Scott thought of me. I went to school as a warrior now, and dedicated my life to getting out of that school alive for the sake of my family. That idea gave me purpose, and in it I found the courage to face each day regardless of what might be coming. I discovered that through not caring what others thought, and through paying attention to simply getting through the day, I was able to survive with little drama.

The boys still bullied me. But as usual, I fought back. That last year I had two fist fights with two different boys, and followed a girl who liked to make fun of me in front of others into a grocery store, where I confronted her and knocked her into a can of vegetables that had been stockpiled on the floor. My attitude was one of "attack and be attacked." As if my feeling knobs had been turned off, I survived that last year of school calmly detached.

I walked home every day by myself. Marc, Leslie, and I never walked home from school together. It was like we weren't even related. In spring of that year, one afternoon after school, Marc showed up in our kitchen with a red stained shirt, with blood dripping fiercely from his nose. He told my mother that Henry had punched him in the face. Henry was a tall doofy boy in my class.

It seemed that the boys in my homeroom had begun picking on my brother, too. Uncertain if it was because of me, I still found myself washed over with guilt. I felt responsible for my brother, although in actuality it was not my fault he got punched in the nose. The sight of him standing there crying as blood leaked from his face filled me with rage.

A few days later, I was walking across 18th Avenue on my way home from school, when I turned to my right and saw what looked like my brother getting pinned up against a brick wall by another boy in my class. Infuriated, I dropped my book bag and began running toward my brother. Ivan had his fist clenched and had steadied himself to land a punch, when he turned and noticed me running at him. Fear came over his face, as he loosened his grip on my brother's shirt and took off running.

Wind carried me swiftly. As I approached Ivan, I slammed both my hands down on his back and swung him around hard, and tossed him against a building's wall. I could feel fury rise within me. My chest heaved. My temper felt almost animal-like as I made a hard fist and cocked my right arm back. I had Ivan's neck pinned against the wall with my left forearm, and I could see myself punching him in the nose like Henry had done to my brother. He was already full of blood, in my mind.

Marc had caught up. I could hear him begging me to hit him. Ivan's eyes grew fearful in obvious anticipation of being slammed in the face by a hairy he/she. As he braced himself for the shot, I loosened my weight on his neck, and dropped my fist. I couldn't hit him.

"You ever, ever, ever, fucking touch my little brother again, I am going to beat the living shit out of you, you piece of shit. Do you hear me? Do you fucking hear me? I swear to God, I will fucking find you, and you won't hear me coming. I will hurt you. I promise you. Don't ever, ever, ever touch him again," I said, as I filled my two fists with his shirt and shoved him roughly up against the wall. "Get your backpack, Marc. We're going home now," I said, as Marc and I, for the fist time, walked home together.

The Summer of 1979

I rode my bike all over town. I loved my blue Schwinn ten-speed, and took very good care of it. Most times I found myself down at the park, canvassing the trails, watching people fish, and hanging out by the water's edge. La Guardia Airport sat across from the park. I enjoyed leaning my forearms over the rusty chain link fence, balancing my weight on my bicycle seat, and watching the big as well as small planes take off and land. The sunsets were spectacular from where I stood. When I closed my eyes, I would focus on the warmth of the sun on my nose, and the sounds the bay made when its body splashed playfully against the huge boulders that stood like guardians around the park's edge.

"Hey, isn't your name Lisa?" she said. Her name was Melanie. She went to my school but was part of another eighth-grade homeroom -- not Scott's, thankfully.

I was leaning over the fence when I heard her call my name. I froze for a moment, unsure what was going to happen next. So accustomed to attack, I held myself back and responded in a nonchalant way, "Yes, why do you want to know?"

"We were just wondering if you wanted to ride bikes with us."

Melanie stood in the center of about five girls. I recognized them all. They all went to my school and were in the same homeroom. I always considered these girls luckier than me, because their class seemed so much more calm and harmonious than mine. It seemed as if my homeroom were full of all the assholes. None of the teachers looked forward to having to deal with my class, and they let us know that. My class was often compared to Melanie's class. It was easy for me, even then, to understand why.

"Ah, no thanks. I have to go home now anyway," I said, as I began to settle myself back onto my bike.

"Well, we ride here every day, so if you want, meet us here tomorrow after school and we'll all ride together," she said.

School was almost over. The year had taken its toll on me, and I had finally arrived at a place where I felt comfortable with my mother's newest label. She had recently begun calling me a "hermit." I looked the word up in the Webster's Dictionary and found that I wasn't offended by the name, like I thought I might have been. I learned to like being alone. I felt less afraid with only my own company.

On the ride home that night from the park, I felt a familiar disturbing feeling begin to surface within me. What if Melanie were nice? What if Melanie were real? What if Melanie really wanted to be friends? What if I tried one more time to be friends with someone? The summer was coming, and maybe, just maybe I could have a great summer this time. School was over, so even if Melanie and her friends hurt me, I wouldn't have to face them again in grammar school. And I'd never have to face the boys in our grade again, even if this was some kind of a set-up … these were the thoughts that cycled through my mind on my way home that night.

It was impossible to get Melanie and her friends out of my head. I remember sitting on my bed, staring out my bedroom window and trying to come up with a plan. I was sure there was a foolproof way to ensure this "friend" thing could work. Honesty and vulnerability had completely blown up in my face. Sharing who I really was with Janice had proven to be an emotional disaster. Being open, direct, and giving had almost destroyed me. There had to be another way to handle people who wanted to get to know me, I thought.

It is saddening even still, for the wise woman I am, who is tapping endlessly at this keyboard, staring deeply into this computer screen, to witness in memory how desperate my child mind was to make and keep a friend. The solution I devised to my dilemma is not one I am proud of. In fact, I still feel the sting of embarrassment, guilt, and shame over how I decided to deal with Melanie and her friends. I am thankful, however, for the spirit being I am; for through my spirit's eyes I find forgiveness for the child's reality I once possessed.

I conjured up what I believed to be a brilliant plan. Instead of revealing my true feelings to Melanie, in the hopes of avoiding ever feeling vulnerable again I decided I would pretend to be the exact opposite of who I was. Instead of coming off as insecure I would lie, and pretend to be who I thought these girls might think was cool. I would become someone I thought they'd want to keep around. Because these girls were not in my homeroom, they knew little about me, so I assumed they didn't yet know that in my class I was considered a loser.

The following day I rode my bike to the park and found Melanie and her friends. Melanie immediately greeted me with a big smile and welcomed me to the group. I tried not to appear nervous as she introduced me to all of her friends. The truth is, I was scared to my bones. They, of course, could never have known that. My demeanor was cool, collected, and controlled. Without yet saying a word, I had already begun to lie.

For whatever reason, Melanie was particularly kind to me. She went out of her way to almost take me under her wing, in this tightly woven group of Catholic schoolgirls. She called me at night to check that I got home, and went out of her way to call my house on Saturday mornings to make sure I was planning on meeting the group to hang out. Melanie's fondness for me made one of the other girls in her group jealous -- so jealous, in fact, that one afternoon in the park, while Melanie and I swung on a metal swing, Leigh thrust the swing next to ours into us as we flew backward and forward in the air. The metal seat hit me in the right side of my head. It took nine stitches to close the gaping wound.

It wasn't long before guilt began feasting on the lining of my stomach. A few weeks into my friendship with these really amazing girls, I had already dug myself into a grave full of lies. I lied about everything. I lied about my relationship with my mother. I told them she and I got along great, and that we shopped together often. I told them that my dad took our family out to dinner once a week, and that we'd gone on lots of family vacations. I told them that I had a rich uncle who was really generous to me. I even lied about things like what my mom made for dinner.

Melanie was not only kind; she was generous, too. My parents saw no need for my siblings and me to have a dollar in our pockets. So when Melanie and the girls got thirsty and wanted to stop for drinks at the corner store, I played down my own thirst, not wanting them to know I didn't have any money. On many occasions, Melanie came out of the store with not one, but two bottles of cold soda -- one for herself, and one for me, the girl who lied about everything.

By the time my mind understood that Melanie and her friends were authentic, and that I didn't need to pretend to be something I wasn't around them, the noose around my neck was already too tight. I told myself I didn't want to lie anymore, and prayed that there was some way I could turn back the clock, and start my friendship with them all over. I felt so ashamed for lying to someone as kind, sweet, and welcoming as Melanie. I hated myself for betraying her.

I had made a conscious decision to stop lying. I distinctly recall being angry with myself for choosing to lie in the first place. All my reasons for wanting to lie seemed as if they'd shot off into the stratosphere somewhere. I couldn't justify one reason now, which only added to the disgust I had for myself.

At the time, I had a huge crush on a boy named Andrew Mc Adams. I liked him not only because he was tall, dark, and handsome, but because he was also an usher at our church. I had gotten into the routine of attending mass every Saturday night just to get a glimpse of his shiny black hair and popping biceps. I can still see him standing there in the aisle, in his dark burgundy short-sleeved dress shirt and dark gray pants. I could have stared at him for days.

It was a steamy night. The girls and I had ridden our bikes for a few hours, and we had just stopped at the 15th Avenue deli for some drinks. I noticed Melanie was particularly quiet, and that Brittany and Christine rode close alongside her, making it impossible for me to ride next to Melanie, like I usually did. When the girls went in to grab sodas, I took off and rode down 124th Street. I was feeling anxious. I knew something had changed among us all, but I wasn't sure what.

As I pedaled feverishly down the street, I bumped into Andrew Mc Adams and his best friend Danny. Startled, but tickled with glee like most young girls are when they bump into their secret beloveds, I raced back to the store to tell the girls that I had found Andrew and his friend. "Guys, guys, guys … guess what? I just bumped into Andrew and Danny. They're down on 124th Street. If we hurry we can find them again," I said, huffing and puffing, hoping they'd all jump on their ten-speeds, and that the chill among us would melt into the steam of the night.

"Sure you did, Lisa. Sure you saw Andrew. Are you sure it wasn't Elvis Presley, or Mickey Mouse you saw down there too?" Brittany said, sarcastically giggling through her words, as she searched Melanie's face for a reaction. Melanie never looked up.

I knew they knew. I knew they knew I was a liar. I knew they had had enough. As my heart sank, and my eyes stung from the consequences of my own actions, I offered this group of deceived girls no apology or explanation. As my vision began to get funnel-like, and my heart thumped wildly in my chest, I plopped myself upon the seat of my blue Schwinn and rode home. There was no one to point the finger at this time, no one to be angry at. I had no one to blame but myself for the pain that was rushing through my veins. I had done this.

I walked my Schwinn into the shed that was nestled into the right corner of our yard, and locked it up. I wouldn't be riding my bike any more that summer. I no longer had any reason to go to the park. I couldn't risk facing Melanie and her friends. I was too ashamed.

I sank into the idea that my summer ended that night. So displeased with what I had done, I decided to punish myself by staying in my room until high school started in September. I found myself more distraught over the fact that I had hurt Melanie than I was embarrassed for all the stupid lies I told. I didn't care that chubby Brittany or carrot-topped Christine made fun of me or knew I had lied. They were never as considerate of me as Melanie anyway. But hurting Melanie made me feel like scum. I'd never felt so ashamed of myself before. This shame I was not confused by. This shame I had brought upon myself, and I was well aware that I had. I was comforted, however, by my mother's opinion of me. It felt right.

My Grand Plan

I watched lots of television that summer, and did my best to stay out of my mother's way. She didn't like seeing me on the couch while she cleaned, so I learned to time my showers and naps around her cleaning regimen. I did lots of thinking, too. Dismayed by the prior two school years, I decided I needed a plan. High school was right around the corner, and in four years I would be gone.

I came to the conclusion that I was better off alone. Making friends had not worked out for me, and I was tired of the pain. I came to accept that my mother and I would never be close, that Marc would always sadly blame me for my parents comparing him to me, and that my father preferred pink elephants to real little girls and boys. Leslie and I weren't close, and I assumed we'd be the kind of sisters who saw each other once a year during the holidays when we got older, if we saw each other at all.

I imagined myself leaving Queens upon graduation, and getting a job in Manhattan. I saw myself alone, in a neat little apartment with a cat or two. I was resigning myself to a life I would spend in solitude. I told myself I would probably work in an office, and be cold to others purposely so no one would try to get close to me. These ideas became the framework I would build my high school experiences on. My agenda was to get in, and get out, with as little contact with others as possible.

I looked forward to the first day of high school. It was the first day of the beginning of my new plan. I liked my plan, and found comfort in its design to keep me protected from others as well as myself. I felt more confident than ever before, because my goals were clear. My intent was to be as cut off from my peers as possible, and to hurry the next four years into my past speedily. I didn't need armor now. No one could hurt me, because I had no intention of giving anyone the chance to.

The first day of school came and went, as did the second, third, and fourth. I was relieved to discover how easy it was not to make friends when I didn't want to. With my plan in full view, I now fought with my mother less, too. I no longer cared whether she approved of me or not. I now disapproved of her, and had decided that once high school was over, we'd have no reason to talk, ever. I learned to accept that my father's true love was money, and that my expecting him to really hear whatever it was I had to say was a waste of time. And although I wished my brother could see how much I cared for him, I had to learn to accept that he'd never be able to see that through his resentment for me. My little sister Leslie was so perfect in my eyes that all I could do was wish her well, and leave her alone. She was doing fine without me messing up her life.

Detachment was feeling really good. Not caring to be cared for offered me a welcome sense of relief from my ever-present anxiety. I never expected my plans to take a nose dive the way they did. My plan was superb, I thought.

Her Name Was Karen

All freshmen were required to do community service. Part of the overall grade a freshman would receive in Religion class would depend on how many hours they volunteered in their communities. I was considering donating my services to the local public library. I'd never seen a smile on any of the faces of the people who worked there. For this reason, I figured the library fit well into my grand plan to get in and get out with as little contact from others as possible, until I was old enough to leave town. My tiny apartment in Manhattan and two cats were waiting.

The all-girls high school I attended was close to my home. I was far less intimidated in high school than I was in grammar school. Certainly, knowing I would not have to deal with boys comparing me to other girls helped ease my fears about starting a new school. Not needing to shield myself in armor, I found myself settling for blinders instead. In a typical school day I'd breathe through each class, with my head looking forward, seemingly unaware of the other girls around me.

My plan was working well. I was growing more comfortable. With each day that passed, I felt more confident that being an antisocial hermit was the right path for someone like me. I learned to accept that I didn't fit in, and grew fonder of the idea that I was probably an alien that had been left behind by my mothership anyway. In my head, I decided that in order to survive my existence on this planet, I'd have to leave it, at least mentally and emotionally, and find another place to exist in until I died.

I was taking my usual stroll home when I heard, "Hey, wait up." I pretended not to hear the voice behind me as I crossed 15th Avenue. Keeping my pace, I didn't look back, not even when I heard, "Come on, wait up. I wanna ask you something. You're in my religion class."

Before the sentence ended, she was standing beside me, a short girl with wavy blonde hair and crystal-blue eyes. Her name was Karen.

"Hi. My name is Karen. Your name is Lisa, right?" I nodded my head, as I began growing icky in my skin. Karen spoke quickly with excitement and with ease, "Have you decided what you're going to do for community service? I wanted to ask you because me and Casey joined the ambulance corps. We made up our own team, but we need one more person to complete it. Oh, by the way, I am not following you. I live on 126th Street. There's my house, actually. Casey lives on 126th Street too. But she's on 22nd Avenue You live on 126th Street at 20th Avenue, right?" I felt bombarded by her firing of questions, and surprised that she knew where I lived. I had never noticed this little girl before.

I didn't know which question to answer first. I didn't want to have to respond to her at all, but she was in my frame of vision, and had chatted the blinders right off my head. "Umm, no … well, I haven't picked a community service option yet," I said.

"Well, there is a meeting tomorrow night for new members at the ambulance corps on 18th Avenue. Me and Casey really like it. It's fun. We are being taught how to do emergency first aid and if we want to, we can eventually ride the ambulance as a first aid responder, and we can even compete in competitions. What do you think?"

The magic question: "What do you think?" Did she really want to know what I was thinking in that moment? My mind swung viciously on a trapeze, while my soul began rubbing sleep from the corners of its eyes. Unsteady on my feet, becoming dazed by this hole Karen just drilled into my escape boat, I decided to not give her an answer until I had my sea legs back. "Can I give you an answer tomorrow? You said you're in my religion class, so I'll tell you tomorrow what I want to do."

Karen walked beside me, talking away, as I listened quietly. Afraid I might say something stupid, or come off unnecessarily hard to this non-intimidating, happy little girl, I kept my mouth shut, and simply waved goodbye as she turned the knob to her front door, and slipped inside. "See ya tomorrow, Lisa," she said.

When you are a child who feels lost in her own skin, everything has the potential to split you open, including the most mundane situations. When you are a child who feels like she has been set on fire, and who is smoldering from the inside out, your eyes cannot help but be on guard for the next dousing of gasoline. When you are a child whose soul is bigger than her head, who has been born into a world that as a whole can see only heads, you feel lost at sea, all your days. When you are a child who cannot help but feel the world around her, who has become intellectually aware that the world around her cannot see her -- it is impossible for a child like this not to make fear her twin.

Looking back, I am saddened at how daunting and overwhelming this simple interaction with Karen felt to me, at the time. Karen, so bubbly, so without reservation, and so open, made me feel as if someone had fanned the flames within me. I had just settled into the comfortable idea that I was in fact a hermit, and would live my life in solitude, detached from having to deal with others. I didn't belong on this planet. I was an alien. I was unlike everyone around me. I was not only unlovable, but deep, deep within me, I had come to the conclusion that I was flawed. The hint in my sense of worth was still just a whisper of dust, and had been all but dissipated by the hate I had for myself since lying to Melanie.

One Day at a Time

I couldn't hear the loud wanting of my soul, but I could feel it. As I walked home that day after meeting Karen, I desperately tried to stop my soul from dancing. My mind had finally been settled, and I had successfully hushed my soul to sleep. My mind was content with its new agenda. From the sense of tapping on my heart, however, it seemed my soul had other plans.

"Hi, Karen," I said as I greeted her in religion class the following day. "I, umm, decided that I'd like to come check out the ambulance corps after all."

The night before, as I lay in bed, I made a few different decisions about the life course I was on. I decided that I would take Karen up on her offer and check out the ambulance corps, strictly for the sole purpose of acquiring the proper credits toward my religion grade. And when that requirement was fulfilled, my relationship with Karen would end. In the meantime, I promised myself I would never lie to Karen about anything, big or small. Although I had no expectations of forming any type of a friendship with her outside the ambulance corps -- my heart so scarred by my deceiving of my other blue-eyed friend -- I made a solemn vow to respect whatever relationship transpired between Karen and me.

The room smelled like fresh Band-Aids. The walls bore faux dark-brown wood paneling, and there were trophies of all sizes in a glass cabinet that sat in one of the corners of the room. The American flag hung from a pole that leaned toward a white extended folding table. Georgia, the director of the youth squad, was sitting on a tan metal folding chair in front of the table. There were a few other kids there my age, but I recognized only Karen and Casey. Casey was in my high-school homeroom.

Georgia was a friendly looking woman with a wide grin. Her eyes were a solid pale blue and her hair was short and prematurely gray. She wore a white uniform shirt with a white turtleneck showing through at the collar. First aid badges covered both shoulders of the shirt. Around her neck was a stop watch on a thick black cord. A tired-looking man named Phil stood beside her. He was Georgia's assistant. Georgia was the director and coach of the volunteer youth squad team.

I kept quiet as I listened intently to what was expected of me as a volunteer. My intent was to do what I had to do, and nothing more. But as the meeting went on, I began to realize that while Goergia would gladly give me her signature so I could pass my religion class requirement, what she really wanted from the kids at the meeting was a commitment to join her competing first aid squad. Karen and Casey had already signed on as members.

When the meeting ended, Georgia made a point to introduce herself to me personally. "Hello. You must be Lisa. Karen told me you were going to join her team. We need only one more person to make the team complete. I think it's wonderful that you decided to join," she said, as she reached for my hand to give it a shake.

So many emotions began to swirl within me. I fought to not bolt for the front door, feeling as if I were beginning to get pulled into relationships I wasn't competent enough to be a part of. I was already anxious about being in the same room with the little blonde girl who knew my name. I was surprised to hear that Karen had already committed me to the team. When I turned to look at Karen,, she stretched her grin widely, and with a childlike voice said, "Pleeeaaaaaaaaaasssssssseeeeeee?"

Unexpectedly, I giggled out loud at the silly face Karen had made as she slowly pronounced the word "please." Laughing was rare for me. Joy, silliness, and happiness were not emotions I was accustomed to. "That's a yes, right? You laughed, so that means you're gonna join, right?" Karen said, as she jumped up and down, reaching out and holding on to my forearm as she bopped into the air. Being touched playfully was also not something I was used to.

"Okay, okay, okay ... I'll join," I said. For the first moment in a long time, I found myself going with the flow in a downward stream. Laughing caught me by surprise and landed me in an emotional spot that felt light -- and better yet, full of possibilities. It wasn't just Karen that I felt good about. I noticed that the ambulance corps members all seemed so uncool. Every person I saw there would have been considered a geek, or a nerd. No one there was particularly beautiful, had a great body, or appeared stuck-up. Georgia was incredibly inviting, and what struck me most about her was how present she was able to make me feel. Neither Karen nor Georgia could have known it, but they had each, in their own way, aroused my interest in living life in a new way. I wasn't sure how things were going to turn out, but for the moment, anyway, I didn't care. Georgia, perhaps sensing vacillation in me, put her hand gently upon my shoulder, patted me lightly, and said, "Don't worry about anything, Lisa ... let's just take this one day at a time."

My Changing View

The following day I found Casey waiting outside my house early in the morning. "Hi, Lisa. Wanna walk to school together?" she asked.

As we walked side by side, and as Casey chatted ferociously about the cute boys who had been at the meeting the night before, all I could focus on was remaining calm. Casey could never have known how foreign I felt in my own skin. Afraid of saying the wrong thing, I remained the listener on our way to our next stop, Karen's house.

Karen was outside waiting for Casey and me. It seemed they met regularly for these morning walks. Antsy, I remained quiet on our walk to school. I could hear my mind talking to itself, warning it not to lie, or act arrogant as I had in the past. My soul danced a jig. I could feel its anticipation rise within me at the promise of new friendships. My mind did its best to balance fear and hope, with just the right touch of detachment. In order for these new friendships to survive, I would need to stay above my fears and unhitched to desperation. As if I were learning to walk for the first time, I told myself not to fall.

I was grateful that Casey was so talkative, and Karen was so aggressive. Between them both, I was able to remain the observer for many weeks ahead. My ideas about the world I was living in were changing fast. The summer before, I had decided to remain a hermit for life. Just a few months later, I was not only making friends, but I was now a member of a competing youth squad team. Like layers of an onion, my notions about others, the world, and even about myself, up and morphed. I was so accustomed to swimming upstream; this new path was awkwardly pulling me forward.

I couldn't see it, but I felt as if I were not alone. As I did my best to ease into these new days, it was as if I had an invisible cheerleader rooting for me inside me somewhere. It was as if there were an older, much wiser part of me coaching me through those delicate days of newness. I'd often hear a voice in my head talking me through anxious moments. The voice told me to relax, be easy, and to loosen up. The voice urged me not to try to be someone or something I was not. And although I did not yet know who I was, the voice gently encouraged me to simply continue going with the flow.

Slowly, my views about my world began to turn around. No longer certain I was going to end up a cat lady in a studio apartment in Manhattan, new ideas sprung up within me as happy emotions began to show up. Learning to be easy wasn't easy. Letting go of what had been was like learning to shed an old layer of skin. I had grown fond of the calluses that had protected me so well, yet I could not ignore the thunderous wanting my soul had for connections to others. In spite of how hard I tried to get my soul to not want, with promise on the horizon, it was impossible to keep my soul asleep now.

It was easier to stay detached from my mother's perceptions of me -- or the perceptions I assumed she had of the person I was -- since the ambulance corps was taking up much of my time now. Georgia requested that we spend at least three nights a week at the ambulance corps, practicing for the upcoming emergency response first aid competition. Karen, Casey, and I were spending more time together on the weekends, and in school we began to meet regularly for lunch in the cafeteria.

I had a long way to go, but in a short time I had come far. I didn't consciously understand at the time how courageous my little girl's heart was. Then, I was simply trying to find a way to squeeze myself into a world that had, in so many ways, in so few years, refused to let me in. By the time I was thirteen, I had resigned the rest of my life to a destiny of aloneness. Life had left me breathless, disillusioned as well as disgusted. Hurt more times than I cared to remember, my battered soul needed to rest. My mind could not have been more stupefied by the resiliency of my being's soul as it awoke once more for a chance at feeling love.

Rosey

Casey was turning thirteen. She was having a sleepover to celebrate. When she invited me, a shiver of self-doubt ran frantically up and down my spine. In spite of the chill, I accepted her invitation. I was apprehensive about attending, because girls I didn't know were going to be there. I had just recently begun to settle into my new friendships with her and Karen. I was anxious about meeting her other friends and having to spend an entire night with them. I had never slept out before.

I walked into Casey's house feeling like a turtle who had its neck stuck out from inside its shell. I was grateful, however, that I didn't feel like a warrior who needed to take up a shield. I'd learned that being quiet was effective at easing my anxiety. When I wasn't talking, I wasn't revealing any of my vulnerabilities; nor was I boasting about things that never happened. Silence was golden, I discovered, and silent I was as Casey's friends came to the door one by one, sleeping bags and pillows tucked neatly under their arms.

There was one girl in the bunch who was quite funny. From the moment she arrived, she was poking fun at herself in a way that had us all in stitches. She was a chubby girl who wore glasses and had extensive acne. I was bowled over by how open this girl named Rosey was about her flaws. At first I was taken aback by her self-deprecating humor. As one routinely swamped by fear of having a flaw exposed, I was struck and almost disoriented by Rosey's way of pointing out what was not perfect about herself.

Rosey's nature was fun-loving, but in her I sensed deep wounds she was trying to heal -- or perhaps expose before anyone else had a chance to. Terribly self-conscious, I had what I considered to be an enormous pimple hiding in the hairline of one of my eyebrows. I worried for two days before the party whether or not any of these girls I didn't even know would notice it. And here Rosey was calling herself names like "crater face" and "dimple thighs" in front of strangers. I was floored.

Eventually I learned to laugh along with the other girls at Rosey's humor. But I couldn't escape the feeling that in poking fun at herself, Rosey was masking pain. By the night's end, Rosey and I had become friends. It was unexpected, for sure, but not without proper reason. Outwardly, Rosey and I had few similarities. On a heart level, however, she and I were more alike than we seemed. Rosey and I both carried deep wounds we needed to protect from further injury. Unlike Rosey, who had decided it hurt less to make fun of her flaws before anyone else did, I, on the other hand, believed in keeping my flaws a secret.

For the first time I instantly felt connected to another human being on a heart level. The feelings I had for Rosey were different from the ones I had for Karen. I didn't understand it then, but I now believe my soul recognized that Rosey and I were wounded in similar ways, and that although I liked Karen and Casey very much, they didn't share the scars Rosey and I did. Neither Rosey nor I knew why we clicked. We just did. As the night progressed, Rosey and I found ourselves laughing out loud together as if we had known each other since birth. I sensed it was impossible for her to be cruel. My heart told me she knew far too well what it felt like to "not feel good enough."

Who, Me?

Life was moving fast in a whole new direction. Our group of three was now a group of four. The following fall, Rosey even transferred to our high school. In a year's time, Casey, Karen, Rosey, and I had become the best of friends. I was spending less and less time at home, enjoying the times I was having with my friends. I was in love with feeling normal, and as if, to these three girls, I were enough.

It was becoming easier to hear my own thoughts without the echo of my mother's disapproval rattling around in my mind. Her opinions of me had become less important as joy began to grow in my heart. Opening my front door to find three girls my age standing there to greet me felt like Christmas morning. Sleepovers became routine, and walking in the rain a complete blast. None of us were gorgeous or would have been considered "hot" by any boy in town, but those kinds of things were never our concern. We all just loved being together.

A few months after Casey's sleepover, Casey, Karen, and I convinced Rosey to join our youth squad team, the "Bumps and Bruises." Each team consisted of five members, one of whom would act as "victim." The victim's job was to lie on the ground and represent the one who had sustained various traumas that needed to be triaged and responded to. Rosey insisted she be our victim, and poked fun at how she didn't think she was very smart, and how she had taken special education classes in grammar school. The victims didn't need to memorize first aid techniques or how to triage. Their jobs were essentially to lie still, and to allow the other four members of the team to bandage them up according to what emergency scenario was given. Rosey welcomed the passive role.

The fifth member on our team was a girl named Carol. She was a year older than we were, and had some prior experience working on another competing squad from our corps. When it came time for Georgia to decide who our team captain was going to be, we all assumed it would be anyone other than Rosey or me, since we were the last two to join the group. Casey, Karen, and Carol had joined the corps much sooner than Rosey or I had. It just made sense that one of three would be given the honorable position.

Georgia had made it a point to make us believe the role of captain was an important one. She also made it known that whomever she chose to be the captain was someone who had impressed her not only with their first aid skill, but with their ability to stay in control under pressure, attention to detail, and leadership qualities. I was flabbergasted when she bestowed the honor on me.

The truth is I wanted to be the captain, and I deserved the role as well. Seeing a chance to shine, I poured many weekend and summer hours into memorizing the *The American Red Cross First Aid Book.*

On some nights, I even skipped hanging out with the girls just so I could study the manual. Georgia tested us often, and I didn't want to disappoint her. Her opinion of me mattered significantly, and in time had grown to be ideas I happily clung to.

It wasn't just the enjoyment I received from hanging out at the ambulance corps with my best friends that made me want to be a part of the Bumps and Bruises. It wasn't just the chance to be around my new crush Vinny, either. My reasons for wanting to be there were much deeper than that.

Georgia was the first woman who had ever taken me seriously. As a matter of fact, she was the first adult in my life who touched me when she didn't have to, and who treated me, from the moment she met me, as if I -- who I was inside -- mattered. Her eyes drew me in, and in the way only a gentle soul can, made me feel welcome, wanted, and appreciated just for being a human being. I fell in love with the way her face found ways to make feel recognized, valid, and even worthy. Georgia, in her innate way, mirrored for me, a sense of good in my "self." In her acknowledgment of me and all my hard work, Georgia had helped lift the veil of invisibility that had for so long covered my soul.

I took the honor of captain to heart. I not only wanted to make Georgia proud, but I also wanted to be someone my teammates could rely on. I grabbed onto my position of leadership, and never looked back. My soul soared at the chance to fly. In our first competition, the Bumps and Bruises took first place in all possible areas. We not only scored higher than all the other youth squads, but we beat out every adult squad as well. In the eyes of the assembly of geeks that gathered in that school gymnasium that day, the Bumps and Bruises were akin to rock stars. Here we were, a group of not-so-pretty young teenage girls from Queens, kicking the asses of all the other much more seasoned volunteer rescue responders. To anyone off the street, this event would have meant little. But to us, and especially to me, it was like winning the lottery.

I never gave my mother the credit she deserved back then. As my interest in volunteering at the ambulance corps grew, I sensed a shift in her perception of me. There was no denying I was important now. In spite of all the times in the past that my mom had found ways to make me feel invalid, my leadership role as well as my growing obvious success in the first aid responders' competition circuit could not be dismissed. What my team had done, no other team in the history of these competitions had ever done. My team was outscoring older, seasoned teams. In addition to sweeping our competitors away, my team won first place in the statewide competitions that were held in the Pocono Mountains. We took home the statewide title three years straight.

I sensed an awkwardness in my mom when I told her about the team practices, the competitions, the fundraising events, and our ultimate wins. I almost didn't tell her Georgia chose me as captain, fearful that on some level, she wouldn't believe I deserved the role. Or perhaps I simply feared feeling that my being captain was unimportant to her. That feeling of being unrecognized was a feeling I didn't want to feel.

It was painful to witness how uneasy she was with her offerings of congratulations. It was always difficult for my mother to look me in the eye, unless she was trying to look through me. I found it perplexing to notice how impossible it was for her soul to look into mine and praise me for a job well done, anytime any job was done well. Through the warmth of my friendships, and through the worthiness Georgia made me feel, letting go of my mother's rift toward me got easier. I never lost, however, the yearning for her to see me entirely. In fact, it is still here.

To my mother's credit, she did try. On various occasions, she volunteered to drive my team to other parts of town to where competitions were being held. They were long days, and for anyone who was not participating in the event, they were tedious and tiring. I loved having my mother come along, in spite of the ghosts that shared our relationship. In spite of all that had been, I wanted her there. I hoped that in her witnessing of me at my best, she'd somehow come to see the best in me. She may never have been able to say it, but I knew Mom wished she could. I knew Mom's heart was chained. I knew she wished it weren't, but it was. And I knew Mom was uncomfortable in her feelings toward me. In all of that, I could sense that Mom was proud of me, and she wished it were easier for her to express that pride on a heart level. However, I was happy that she just showed up.

My Parents Were People Too

My heart was no longer the parched well it once was. I had learned my lessons and learned them well -- at least the lessons I was supposed to learn thus far. The little pudgy girl I had met that first day of camp was right. If you want people to like you, you have to be nice. I came to understand, at least on a heart level, that in order to have friends, you have to be a friend first. God, the universe,whatever, had given me plenty of opportunities to make friends. My lack of self-worth, however, hung on my nose like a "no vacancy" sign. It wasn't anyone else's fault that I thought my life sucked.

My new friends were like lifesavers, literally. My heart, once full of dark lonely space, was finally beginning to fill up with light. With every sleepover, every giggle, and every trip to the local roller rink, I found myself growing seeds of joy within me. The new glee in my heart was like a long arm. No longer feeling like I was caught up in the vortex of a vicious tornado, love blessed me with the ability to detach from my attachment to the deep wounds I suffered at the cost of never feeling truly loved on a heart level. This awe-inspiring new height in my mind allowed me to look beyond my own pain, and to see my parents for more than the blame I had assigned to them.

When your heart feels like it's hemorrhaging, its all but impossible to be grateful for the chest cavity that contains it so perfectly. The delight I found in the silliness of friendships helped me to stop my heart from bleeding, and as the blood flow slowed, room was made for more good feelings. The more my heart filled with joy, the greater its wanting became for more joy. It was impossible for me to hold on to anger any longer. I craved love now, like a wolf craved meat.

My perceptions of life and the people in it were changing rapidly. Although a piece of my heart still ached for a deep, connected, authentic relationship with my mother and father, I was learning to accept them for who they were, in spite of how many times I had felt rejected by them. I questioned, too, whether they had ever truly rejected me, and pondered whether, in truth, they were simply unable to relate to me on a heart level? As the pain in my heart subsided, I was able to push past old ideas, and over the carcasses of old beliefs.

My mother was easing up on me. I could feel it. There was still a chilliness between us; however, I no longer felt as if her nails were digging into the back of my neck. Not needing to feel so guarded around her, I was able to see with a larger eye how much my mother's life had been about personal sacrifice. It wasn't her fault, either, that her life sucked. And although my mother would never admit that she wished her life were different, in my heart stood a strong convicted knowing that she did. Deeper, although I knew my mother would never look me in the eye and say it, I sensed she was sorry for what had been between us.

I learned to see past the weaknesses I saw in my father, too. It wasn't his fault he couldn't feel. I could imagine what he felt like as innocent little boy, on the day his young beautiful Italian mother chose to end her life, and I didn't enjoy what I felt. My father was a victim of a lack of self-love. His mother's inability to love herself to her core robbed him of the chance ever to feel safe enough to open his heart again. So crippled by the fear of abandonment, my father till this day refuses to expose himself to vulnerability.

My parents loved us in ways that they themselves were not loved as children. Their ideas of love had little to do with words, hugs, or appropriate praise. My mother loved me when she was making certain my clothes were clean and ironed. She was loving me when she showed up on time for a parent- teacher meeting. She was loving me when she took me into the city to have my retainer adjusted. She loved me when she found the money each Christmas to buy me the one present I asked for. My mother loved me by not drinking.

My father wasn't the type to show up at my school play or tell me I was beautiful. But he was the type of dad who found time on a Sunday morning to take my brother, sister, and me to the park to play hide and seek. He wasn't the kind of dad who encouraged me to tell him how I felt, but he was the kind of dad who worked seven days a week so I could go to private schools. He wasn't the kind of dad who was generous with hugs, but he was the kind of dad who made sure I was safe. My father showed his love by never abandoning me.

The innocent children my parents were deserved better. As love for friends and their love for me softly fanned the flames of my soul, I found myself learning to love my parents as people, instead of just as a mother and a father. As love blossomed, it gobbled up old pangs like ivy takes over a meadow. It was glorious, and tart at the same time. These latest shifts in perceptions of my world and the people in it needed to sit upon a shelf in my ever-expanding awareness. These ideas I could not share. No one would have understood them anyway. I was learning to be okay with that.

An Amazing Chance

I knew what she was doing. Casey was lying. I never called her out on it. I didn't want to hurt or embarrass her the way Brittany had done to me. Karen, and Rosey knew she was lying, too. The three of us had discussed her lying a number of times. Karen and Rosey thought we should confront her and tell her we knew. I urged them to ignore her, and let her talk.

Casey lied about everything. At least it seemed like she did. On our walks to school, which now included Rosey, she would tell wild fables about dreams she had had, and about people she was "just happening to meet" when she wasn't hanging out with us. Casey's parents were going through a hard time in their marriage. Casey told us she thought her father might be having an affair. In my heart, I assumed that Casey's fantasies helped take her away from what was going on at home, like my lies had taken me away from my fears of not being enough.

The four of us regularly roller skated at the local rink in Flushing Meadow Park. Much to my surprise, I was very good at skating. I loved the loud music, the flashing lights, and the energy of the people around me. Skating came naturally to me. I could sense that Casey was envious of how well I could skate. Karen and Rosey sensed it too. It wasn't just the fact that Casey talked her mom into letting her take private skating lessons and didn't tell us about it that caused us to question how Casey was feeling. Casey started wearing the same kinds of clothes I wore, and made it a point to try and spend time alone with me, away from Karen and Rosey.

At times it was difficult not to confront Casey. My intent would never have been to humiliate her, or express anger toward her. I could sense Casey's infatuation with me growing, judging by how often she was calling me and suggesting we spend time together that did not include Rosey or Karen. Rosey and Karen, on the other hand, were growing less tolerant of her wild stories about boys who were trying to date her, as well as her attempts to manipulate me. Karen and Rosey were taken back by how understanding and non-angered I was by Casey. I wished I could tell them that not so long ago, I was very similar to Casey.

It was the end of second period. A new friend we had met in sophomore year named Anna had joined our small group of misfits. Anna fit right in. She was a heavy girl with beautiful skin, dazzling light- brown eyes, and the most flawless skin I had ever seen in my life. Anna was opinionated, intelligent, friendly, and held nothing back when it came to confronting issues head-on. As Karen and Rosey shared what was going on with Casey and her increasingly bizarre behavior toward me, Anna was free with her obviously pissed-off take on things.

Anna made it known that she thought I should confront Casey about her lies, as well as about her trying to snuff Rosey and Karen out of the exclusive imagined loop she was trying to create between herself and me. It seemed like the more passive I was about confronting Casey, the more adamant Anna grew. As we both stood in front of our lockers at the end of second period, Anna told me she got a glimpse of a picture Casey had in her wallet, while Casey was paying for her lunch on the cafeteria line that morning. It was a picture of a girl and a boy skating backwards at the Pavillion in Flushing Meadow Park. You could not make out who the girl in the photo was, because her face had been darkened by a black marker.

I was unconcerned about the photo, and felt myself growing irritated at Anna for the way she was pushing her agenda on me. I felt resolved, however, in my decision not to hurt Casey's feelings regarding her lying. In my mind, I hoped it was just something she'd feel compelled to stop doing, the same way I felt before Brittany confronted me in the humiliating way that she had. Way before Brittany called me out in front of Melanie and the rest of the girls that hot steamy night, guilt had already spun my heart and head around. Of my own volition, I had decided to stop lying to Melanie and her friends. Sadly, however, for me it was already too late. I kept holding on to the hope that Casey too, would feel the desire to stop lying on her own before any of us felt the need to confront her.

"Lisa, the girl in the picture is you. Casey blacked your face out with a marker and is telling everybody that the girl is her. Remember that night that guy asked you to skate? Remember the really tall guy Albert? Remember the white shirt you had on, and the tan pants you were wearing when we all went there like three weeks ago? Well, that night Casey had her camera ... remember? And the picture she took of you when you were skating backwards with that guy is the picture I am talking about. Casey is telling her friends from other classes that she is the one in the picture, that that is her boyfriend. She is telling everyone she didn't like the way she came out in the picture and that's why she had to black out the face. Well! Well! Are you going to do anything now?! Casey is going crazy, and you know it, and you won't say anything. She isn't obsessed with me, or Rosey, or Karen. She's obsessed with you, and now you have to do something. This has gone too far," Anna angrily spewed.

"Look, I know you guys all want me to confront her," I said. "I get that, but I am not going to confront her unless I see that picture."

"Okay -- I'm gonna steal the picture so you can see it. THEN will you do something about her lying?" Anna pushed me for an answer.

Anna was right. The girl in the photo was me, and she had blackened my face out just like Anna said. Rosey, Karen, and Anna stood in front of me and waited for me to respond, as I held the picture in my hand. While Casey fetched french fries off the cafeteria line, Anna had slipped into Casey's unattended wallet and retrieved the photo without Casey knowing. I couldn't be angry. I couldn't say anything harmful about Casey. I had not an ounce of revenge or disgust in me for what she had done. Sadness engulfed me instead.

My friends were right. I had to do something. But they were wrong about what it was they thought I had to do. I didn't want to lose Casey as a friend, like I had lost Melanie. I didn't want Casey to feel like she had to be ashamed when she looked at me. I wanted us to be closer than ever, in spite of what she had done. I wanted her to know that I understood why it might have been that she told stories, exaggerated, and pretended to be someone she wasn't. My greatest desire was to spare her the humiliation I had experienced when I was not being as truthful as I should have been. In an amazing, telling, and miraculous twist of fate, in this scenario between Casey and me, I was her Melanie. In my mind, even at that young age at the time, I saw what was happening as a chance to heal not only Casey, but a part of my past as well.

I took the picture from Anna, and walked to an empty classroom. I had the next two periods free, so I decided to sit down and write Casey a letter, instead of confronting her head-on. She and I shared the same homeroom. Both our names began with the letter C. I wrote the letter and slipped it into her locker so she'd get a chance to read it alone before I got to homeroom. I didn't want her to have to deal with worrying about me standing there, possibly judging her as she absorbed what I had written. It was important to me to treat her with dignity through this tangled web of sad, unfortunate tales.

Dear Casey,

I want to start this letter off by telling you how great I think you are. You, Rosey, Karen, and Anna, are the best friends I have ever had. You have been especially kind to me. You call for me in the rain, and always remember to bring me things from your trips out with your mom and grandma. I just want to say thank you for being you and for inviting me to your sleepover when you hardly even knew me. It was there that I met Rosey, and really started to feel close to you and Karen.

I am sorry that I had to write this letter. And I am sorry

that Anna stole this picture out of your wallet. I need you to know that I am not angry at all. I have no hard feelings for you, and I hope you know that to be true in your heart. I love you and think you're great in spite of all this.

I want you to understand that I understand why sometimes we feel the need to escape our lives through the telling of lies. I want you to understand that I too have felt the need to pretend to be someone else at times. My life isn't and has never been an easy one. I have hated myself and have questioned why I was ever even born. I always felt like I didn't fit in or belong here. I have even wanted to die, because I felt so alone. Lies can be like canoes for us sometimes. They take us away from the pain of what is, and help float us to somewhere less frightening, less frustrating, and less confusing. We don't realize it at the time, but although lies help our minds escape, the truth is, they always mess up what is. Eventually the canoe has to return home, and when it does, we find that we really didn't escape anything. All the anger, fear, frustration, and disappointment are right there on the shore, waiting for us to come home.

I don't care about the fibs. I don't care about the picture. And I don't care what you have done. I swear, I hope you believe me. I have nothing in my heart for you but understanding, and empathy, and forgiveness. People who lie don't lie because they're happy. People who lie are sad, afraid, lonely, desperate, and even insecure. My intent is not to make you feel worse, but better. I want you to know that I love you with my heart, in spite of all of this silliness. It means nothing to me, and all I want is for us to get closer because of it, and to never grow apart because of it.

Please, Casey, don't ever feel ashamed or embarrassed when you look at me. Know in your heart that I have already forgotten all of this. It is as if it never happened, in my mind.

Sometimes we need a wake-up call to help us realize when we are messing up our lives. I hope this was it for you. You will always be very dear to my heart. And I want to thank you for giving me an opportunity to be loving, caring, and understanding. I am also quite flattered. I never ever imagined anyone would ever be envious of little old quirky me. I am not sure what it is you see in me that you admire. But I am humbled by your feelings toward me. You should know, though, that if you see me as someone who is strong, that is only because for so long I felt wrong. When I stopped trying to impress others, hoping they'd like me, and instead learned to just be me, God gave me all of you.

Casey, you're enough. Please just be yourself around me. And don't ever feel like you need to be anything more than who you are....

Lisa

Casey was crying when I walked into homeroom that day. The letter I wrote her was still in her hands. She ran to me, and with open arms, she crumbled into mine. As I wrapped my arms around her, I felt a holiness wash upon us both. In my mind, this could not have been anything short of a miracle. I was in awe at the chance I had been given to heal such a deep wound in me, through the forgiving of Casey. I needed Casey to understand that I was thankful for the chance not only to forgive her, but to also forgive myself for lying to Melanie. I came to realize that what I saw in Casey, I needed to see and also forgive in myself. For too long I had gone on hating myself for lying to Melanie and her friends. I understood now that I hadn't lied because I was bad; I lied because I was afraid of being less than who others might have thought I was.

All Casey could do was whimper, and through a mouthful of tin repeat over and over how sorry she was. I didn't want nor did I need her apology. I had been guilty of the same offense. I did not feel I had the right to judge her or to stand in conviction of her. Regardless of how many times I tried to tell her not to feel bad or guilty, she could not help but feel ashamed. Casey and I drifted apart from that day on. She stopped walking to school with Rosey, Karen, and me, and eventually quit the ambulance corps, too. At lunch, she found a new group of girls to hang out with, and in time our friendship was reduced to a simple nod of acknowledgment in the school hallways.

It wasn't the way I had hoped things would turn out between Casey and me. For my own selfish reasons, I suppose, I wanted the opportunity to be kind to her after I confronted her. I saw the two of us as two peas in a pod, who had overcome our personal insecurities through a real friendship that had its roots in forgiveness. I craved the kind of honesty and compassion Casey and I now shared, and secretly prayed we'd be able to manage a friendship into the future. In the end, I knew I needed to understand why Casey had to break away. I knew it might be harder for her to forgive herself than it was for me to forgive her.

Lost and Found
Found and Lost

Things were going really well for me at the ambulance corps. I felt so alive when I was there in that wide-open room that smelled like Band-Aids. With each new day, I was falling more in love with how lit-up the feelings of satisfaction, appreciation, safety, and acceptance could make me feel. Being a member of the Bumps and Bruises made me feel like I belonged to something. The honor of being made captain only sweetened my experience there.

Georgia had managed to pull together a second competing youth squad from our corps. They called themselves the "Stretcher Fetchers." While Bumps and Bruises was an all-girls team, the Stretcher Fetchers was an all-boys team. The captain of that team was a tall, lanky boy who had a large nose with a hump in the middle of it. He had hair as black as night, and eyes that were a deep cocoa brown. His skin was Mediterranean, and obviously oily. He seemed very proud of the stethoscope he wore around his neck, and the number of first aid patches on his sleeves. His name was Vinny.

I noticed Vinny the night I met Georgia for the first time. He was sitting on the edge of the table to her left, one cheek on, and one cheek off, his one leg dangling above the floor as he waved his foot in the air back and forth. I sensed that he enjoyed what he did there. He had a cool sense about him, or at least it seemed as if he wanted all of us who were there for the meeting to see him that way. I didn't think he was gorgeous, as I had once thought Scott was, but I liked him anyway. I got the feeling Vinny was a misfit too, despite the effort he put into trying to convince others he wasn't.

Right before my fifteenth birthday Vinny asked me to go out with him. Rosey, Karen, and Casey had suggested that they thought he liked me. I was hesitant to believe them, still too insecure to think any boy would really like me in a boy-girl kinda way. Although my body had naturally transformed itself, and I was no longer flat-chested or looked like a boy from behind, the schema I had of my body image, in my mind's eye, was far from positive.

On the night of February 15th, 1980, Vinny asked if he could walk me home from the ambulance corps. I usually walked home with Karen, Casey, and Rosey, but on this night, Vinny asked my friends if it would be all right if he walked me home instead. I remember feeling immediately light-headed, and as if I were in a fog. It almost didn't feel real.

A few blocks from my house, Vinny stopped, turned toward me, and looked me in the eye. He was nervous and fussing with his hands. It was a cold February night, and little puffs of white breath could be seen making their way out of our mouths. I was so nervous I thought I might pee my pants. "I really like you, Lisa, and I was wondering if you'd go out with me?" he asked anxiously, unable to keep still in the bitter cold. My heart thumping hard enough for the both of us, I said, "Yes, I'd like that very much." We both giggled and looked down at the ground a few times, before he shyly reached for my hand. As his hand took mine, a rush of teenage sexual attracting power flooded my veins. If I were a butterfly, this was the night I was born.

It was difficult for me to contain my excitement. My lips were quivering and my muscles were shaking, more from the adrenaline that was flooding my nervous system than from the harsh winter wind. Of course I blamed my involuntary movements on Mother Nature. My feet high above the ground, I grew increasingly anticipatory of our first kiss. I had never French kissed a boy, and was slightly terrified at the thought of sticking my tongue into Vinny's mouth. I wondered what I'd do when he tried to slip his wet tongue into my mouth. It was uncomfortable to think about, and I worried I'd think it was gross when he tried. As we approached the corner where I lived, my heart began to do a jig. I could almost feel the kiss waiting for me on my stoop.

This newness was coming at me fast. Amidst the joyous births of butterflies in my belly, shadows of self-doubt struggled to rear their ugly heads. I could feel my old thought patterns wanting me to fall. Luckily, the excitement of suspense held me still long enough to allow the cosmos to take over when Vinny leaned in close to me, and gently slipped his thin tongue across my lips and into my mouth. It was not a long kiss. I was thankful Karen had told me how to "make out," just in case she were right and Vinny really did like me. My mind screamed inside itself, hoping neither Mom nor Dad had seen Vinny and me kissing at the front door.

Vinny's haste told me he was relieved the kiss was over, as was I. The kiss felt more like a fine detail we needed to get past than romantic or lustful. The truth is that I was terrified by the idea of having to kiss Vinny. I felt awkward in my own skin, and doubted I would kiss him the right way, if there were a right way to tongue kiss. I liked Vinny very much. I sensed we shared more than just the titles of "Captain" in common.

That night, as I lay in my bed, and pulled the crocheted multi-striped yarn blanket my mother had made over my shoulders, I thanked God I hadn't killed myself when I was twelve. Happy emotions surged, while throbbing memories of old flashed like movie clips in my mind's eye. It was surreal to recall how desperate I had once felt, not so long ago. The contrast between my past and my now – it was so harsh; my feelings could not help but be bittersweet. I found myself weeping not only out of thankfulness, but out of grief as well, for the innocent lost little girl I was, who had once been convinced she was nothing.

Head Over Heels

Vinny and I were officially boyfriend and girlfriend. I wasn't sure what that meant, but I was enjoying feeling special. Having a boyfriend made me feel wanted. Having a boyfriend made me feel like I was wearing a sign on my forehead that read, "Look at me, everybody ... you see ... somebody thinks I'm worth something ... somebody loves me ... somebody needs me....You see, I really do matter..." At the time, I thought that was a good thing. At the time, because I still had lots of unresolved issues to sort out, I was unaware of how much of my personal worth I had placed into the hands of another flawed human being.

The first few months of our relationship felt like a dream. I became so preoccupied with thoughts about Vinny that it was impossible to concentrate on my grades. Achieving was no longer high on my list of wants. All I wanted to do now was be with Vinny. In school, I would write poems about how deeply I cared for him, and how lucky I felt to have such an amazing boy in my life. I wrote about how lost I felt until he asked me to be his girlfriend, and how I prayed our relationship would never end. I'd run home from school and dash to the phone, eager to hear his voice at the end of a tedious school day. And sadly, more times than I'd like to recall, I blew off plans with my girlfriends just to be with him.

Vinny was quiet with his feelings, but usually found ways to let me know he was thinking about me just as much … at least in the beginning of our relationship, that is. He would leave tiny love notes in my backpack, or slip them into my coat pockets. He would leave roses on my stoop, and often bought me romantic cards and tiny trinkets. It was impossible to hold on to my heart. Vinny's attention was like water to my dehydrated soul. Vinny touched me on a level that my new girlfriends never could have. It was a spot that felt very close to where I housed the desire to be loved by my mom and dad. The feelings that burst open in me for Vinny felt as if they were rising forth from my toes. And when he reciprocated with his affection and attention, it was as if I were entering into this atmosphere for the first time, time and time again.

A few months into our relationship, Vinny was all my mind could think about. I struggled with finding balance in my suddenly full and ever-expanding life. I was aware that I was spending less time with Rosey and Karen, and that my schoolwork had taken a sudden back seat. Rosey and Karen were blatantly honest, and let me know they thought I was spending too much time with Vinny. I was beginning to feel overwhelmed, and as if I were losing the very filaments of the self I had just begun to find. When I wasn't thinking about how to please Vinny, I was worrying about how not to upset my friends. I was losing ground quickly, and sinking back into old patterns of thought I had learned as a child. But because the characters in my life were all new and so different, the old patterns took me very much by surprise.

I wanted it all, now. I wanted Vinny and I wanted my friends, and although my attention to my schoolwork had diminished, I wanted high grades, too. I didn't want just to compete in the youth squad games. I wanted to win. And I didn't want just to win. I wanted to win first place. I didn't want first place overall -- I wanted first place in every game, too. And I didn't want just to sweep first place in the youth division. I wanted to sweep first place over the adult squads as well. As if breathing life into my lungs for the first time, my desires for more sprung forth ferociously and with vigor.

I was still too young to know how destructive my seemingly wonderful life really was. As I look back, heavy sighs make their slow way out of my much older lungs. It is all so clear now; I am amazed by how scarring and elusive love can be. Or shall I say, how scarring what one learns to define as love can be. When I was throwing my books on my bed, and dashing to Vinny's house a few blocks away because he was timing me to see how quickly I could get there after school, I believed I was loving him. When Vinny took off from work early, and called me to come over and I ditched Rosey and Karen to meet him, I thought I did that because I loved him. And when I found myself unable to think about anything else but how to please him, I believed that too was love.

About a year into our relationship, I felt our relationship change. I was stunned and deeply hurt when Vinny made his first negative comment about my weight. He implied I should drop a few pounds, and told me to consider eating salad more often. It made me feel as if I were suddenly not good enough for him, and as if he were placing less value on me because of my weight. I was five foot seven and perhaps one hundred and thirty pounds at the time. Soon after he started commenting about my weight, he began making negative comments about my hair. He didn't like how "thick" it was, and told me he wished it looked more like another girl's hair.

Our relationship changed dramatically after Vinny's first year of college. While he had always had an air about him, he seemed to grow increasingly arrogant and pompous once he was in college. He seemed to enjoy speaking to me about "all the college girls" he had met since he had enrolled. He'd smile his way through telling me about the lunches he would share in the cafeteria with his new classmates, and how he had even driven a few home from class. Vinny was studying to be a nurse, and at the time, he was the only male in the program.

It was growing more difficult to ignore the way Vinny was changing. At competitions, he would ignore me as if I didn't exist, and talk to pretty girls on other teams. Back at the ambulance corps, he would deny he had ignored me, and tell me it was all in my head. He would accuse me of being insecure, and tell me I was crazy. He would insist it wasn't his fault if girls talked to him, and that I was being unreasonable. On more than one occasion he told me that if I lost some weight and did my hair differently, that I would feel better about myself, and probably wouldn't worry so much about whom he spoke to.

I thought I loved Vinny. And I thought that love meant sticking it out no matter what, even if the person I loved was hurting me with his words and behavior. In a very short time, and unbeknownst to me consciously, I willingly awarded Vinny the role of boss over me. More concerned with feeling "accepted, validated, and worthy" by another human being, I lost sight of the glimpse of "self-love, self-acceptance, and self-worth" I was just beginning to discover before I started dating Vinny. The romantic feelings I had for this boy took me over, as if in my mind, he was to heal every psychic wound I had ever suffered as a child, long before I ever knew he existed.

Vinny and I were together on and off for almost six years. We dated steadily for three, while it took almost as long to disentangle ourselves from the elusive web our relationship became. We fought often. Our relationship evolved into a roller coaster of ups and downs. When we were up, it felt like I was floating on a cloud, and as if some kind of mood-elevating drug had lifted me there. But when we were down, it felt as if my entire world teetered on the top of a pin, and as if the slightest shift to the left or to the right world cause my world to stumble and crash to the ground. My feelings for Vinny consumed me. All too quickly, the self I had just recently come to know began to fade.

I dated Vinny until my third semester in college. During those years, our relationship was more off than it was on. Once in college, I found myself surrounded by the opposite sex, most of whom were more than happy to get to know me better. By the time I turned nineteen, my body blossomed. I was no longer a lanky, frizzy-haired, awkward teenage girl; time somehow managed to help ease me into a more feminine, attractive being. When I was sixteen I traded my old-fogey glasses for contacts. I also studied fashion magazines for tips on make-up and hairstyles. While I wasn't what most would consider drop-dead gorgeous, I could no longer be mistaken for a boy, not even by a long shot.

The attention I got at college took me by surprise. Vinny and I went to the same school. When we'd pass each other on campus on our way to our own classes, Vinny never went out of his way to acknowledge me. The boys who were in classes with me would inevitably point out my boyfriend's disregard toward me. More than once, different boys told me that, from their point of view, as a male, Vinny had no respect for me. They also told me that someone as pretty and as nice as I was should not tolerate being treated that way.

Anthony was an Italian boy from my English class. One day while I waited in the rain for a bus to take me back home after English class, Anthony stopped his car in the street and motioned for me to come to the passenger's side window. As rain found its way down the back of my neck through a space in my shirt, I leaned into Anthony's white boat-sized Monte Carlo. "What are you doing in the rain? Get in. I'll drive you home."

On the way to my home, Anthony asked me all sorts of questions about Vinny. "Does your boyfriend drive? Why didn't your boyfriend wait for you after his last class and drive you home? Why does he act like he doesn't know you when he sees you? Why do you tolerate him ignoring you? Doesn't it bother you that he drives other girls home but has never driven you home? You're not thinking of marrying that asshole, are you? Why are you wasting your time with someone who treats you like shit, and pretends to not even notice you on campus?" Anthony's questions stung me like a wasp between my eyes.

Anthony was right, and so were Sal, Gerard, Jimmy, and Raphael. I had met all five of these boys in various classes of mine that first year of college, and all of them felt the same way about my situation. As hard as I tried to deny it, the truth was that as much as I loved Vinny, he didn't deserve my love. I broke up with Vinny for good just around the time I turned twenty. It was one of the most difficult decisions I ever had to make. In spite of the fact that I had lost myself inside our relationship, on a deep level I knew I deserved better. I ended my relationship with Vinny, but not because I didn't love him. I ended my relationship with Vinny because although I believed Vinny loved me, he could not love me very much.

Big Girl Addictions

When I was a little girl, I soothed myself by way of writing out my fantasies. Paper, like giant indigo peacock feathers built for one, swooped me up and carried me away from places that were far too scary for little girls. Trapped and lost inside my own mind, the walls I lived within bore no mirrors. Was I good? Was I real? Did I matter? Was I worthy? Were my feelings valid? Was I valid? Writing helped to purge the poison that grew from feeling invisible. Eventually, my mind found other ways to ease its anxiety. Counting, memorizing, and pulling hairs from my head, although they sound like insane types of behavior, in truth kept my psyche from splintering. Like apron strings sewn to my soul, I hung on to its sleeping self, regardless of how deep its state of slumber, awaiting the day it would finally awaken and look me in the eye.

Vinny and I had no real future. And although I knew that consciously, my heart still ached. Like a phantom limb, I felt him although he was gone. Everywhere I looked and everything I did reminded me of him. In fact, he was always on my mind. Like a fossil etched in my neurons, Vinny was just there.

Vinny was out of my life, but the residual feelings I held for him remained. So accustomed to the routine that became ours over the years, it was difficult for me to break the habits I had come to know. As unworkable as our relationship had become, it was all I knew. The ups and downs had become commonplace. As dysfunctional as we were, it was what I was comfortable with. True, the belly of our problems was simply a manifestation of all that was not right within both of us. We just didn't know that then. Each of us, so riddled with insecurities, used the other to mask what we both hated in ourselves. We both felt unlovable, and each found a way to get the other to be responsible for that lack. While Vinny played on my insecurities to build himself up, in an effort to boost his ego and therefore override his own lack of self-worth, I begged for his acceptance of me in the hope that in his validation of me, the black stains on my soul would be washed clean. Neither of us was yet responsible for our own sense of worth, so each manipulated the other, instead of turning our eyes within.

Like a long locomotive that was now missing a bunch of its boxcars, my mind felt as if something was amiss. So accustomed to running its twisted, but reliable path, my mind felt confused and lost, uncertain of how to fill the empty spaces. Worse, the contents of my boxcars were still there, in spite of the fact that my boxcar Vinny was not. Unsure of what to do with all of the "icky" feelings, my mind did what it always did when stressed. It found something else to control, to offer me a false sense of power over my own life.

While sitting in the seat of retrospection, I am washed over by humility at how many murky abysses I have had to face and quell in my life. Each dark gap felt as if it were the darkest I had yet faced, and yet the holes continued to show up on my journey as I triumphed on. Believing I was learning the lessons along the way, I sit here stymied by how little I was actually learning, and how much I still had to learn. I was very proud that I had finally found the courage to end my relationship with Vinny for good, and I believed that I thought well of myself for doing so. But the reality was that as a conscious part of myself struggled to hold on to the feeling of self-pride, another deeper and unconscious part of me shivered in fear. Alone -- or so I felt -- the most wounded part of me did not know how to deal without its dysfunctional counterpart. My wounds needed someone to pick their scabs and to put them back on. I didn't know how to function without blaming someone else for my lack, or to praise someone for when I felt full.

For the next two years, I fell into what I can only describe as a cesspool of illusions. A big girl now, I was concerned about how I looked to others. I was aware of how my body had changed, and that these changes were catching the attention of boys and men. And although in many ways I felt good about the attention I received, on a deeper level I was ambivalent about it. Duality once again reared its challenging head, as I muddled through this turbulent terrain. I began obsessing about the way that I looked, and especially how much I weighed. The message I received from the outside world was that the thinner I was, the more attention I received. The more attention I received, the more value I believed I had. And so the loop began.

It started out innocently enough. After I broke up with Vinny, I began jogging. I heard myself say that I wanted to lose just a few extra pounds. Although my conscious intentions were good, my unconscious patterned thoughts had another agenda. I needed a wild horse to tame. I needed something for my mind to obsess about as I played out my role as a physical being. While my social life, school life, and family life continued on, in the places no one else even knew existed in me, my mind clung to its need to obsess, latched on to my good intentions, and lit them ablaze.

For the next two years, I found myself slowly sinking into a love/hate relationship with food and exercise. If I wasn't grossly restricting my calories, I was feasting on them instead. And when I wasn't praising myself for doing such a good job at starving myself, I was guilting myself for eating. I couldn't do forty-five crunches. I had to do 2500. I couldn't skip just one meal. Instead, I had to prove to myself I could go without solid food for a day, or two or three. I told myself it was good to give my digestive system a rest, and to fast to purify my body. I told myself there was nothing wrong with skipping meals, as long as I drank tea with sugar, and remembered to drink orange juice and water. My mind no longer had time to crave Vinny. It was too busy obsessing about what not to eat, what I could eat, and when the hell I was going to find the time to exercise off the calories I ate when I did eat.

I had found a new boxcar to stuff all my anxiety into. My mind was now back on its peculiar track. I could function this way -- at least outwardly, that is. Without a place to stuff the anxiety that was the result of my learning to believe in my unworthiness as a child, my mind felt as if it were missing a wheel. I had to have some place to house the ghosts, the whispers, and the ills. As college strolled on, my mind existed in two places at once, or maybe three. While I wrote impressive nursing care plans, and dispensed medications to my patients, I could hear the taped recording repeating itself over and over in the shadows of my mind. It reminded me to count my calories at lunch, and to drink only water. It told me to drink orange juice if I felt faint, and recalled new exercises I could try once I got home. It prompted me to suck in my abs at all times, and to isometrically squeeze my biceps during nursing lectures. And every time I almost forgot to think about food, it jogged my mind to remember I wasn't yet enough.

The First White Flag

I began dating other boys immediately after Vinny and I broke up. I even went on a few dates with Anthony. I casually dated a few other boys at school, and even dated the local and very popular, very Polish pizza guy from our town. I was taken aback by how many boys were interested in me once Vinny and I broke up. It was a far cry from my grammar school days, when the boys of way back when weren't even sure I was a girl.

I met Steven when I was twenty-one. I remember walking past a new building that was going up on Main Street, and seeing him in a hole in the building, where the front windows were going to be installed. His father's construction company had been contracted to renovate the building. He was tall, deeply tanned, and shirtless. I noticed the moment he noticed me, and felt attracted to him instantly. I was working two jobs at the time. During the week I worked at a pharmacy, and on the weekends I worked in a deli. One hot Saturday morning, Steven came into the deli where I worked as a cashier, to buy cold bottles of water for himself and his workers.

Steven seemed shy. I found that attractive. So often I had found men staring at me as if I were a succulent entrée. Stuck behind a cash register, I would feel trapped and violated as various men on my check out line ogled my boobs or gazed at my crotch. I hated when two or three men on my line would whisper to one another as they each took glances my way. It would send nauseating chills down my spine when men fondled their family jewels as they passed me their money. Most customers of the deli were blue-collar working men looking to buy their breakfast and lunch. But the ogling was not an exclusive trait of theirs. I found that white-collar men ogled just as much. They were just sneakier about it.

Steven's reserved demeanor was refreshing. His intimidation surprised me and piqued my interest in him. I was pleased by his coy disposition, because in truth, if any of the men who had ever stood in my line should have been cocky, he should have. He was an Italian Adonis, and I liked that he didn't know it.

Steven became a regular in the deli while his dad's company worked on the building across the street. When he showed up on a Sunday morning in a clean t-shirt and a nice pair of jeans, I knew he was interested in me. He didn't work on Sundays. It took him six months to finally ask me out, three months after he originally had asked me for my number. The weekend he found the courage to call my house and ask me out on a date, I had all but given up on him. In fact, that very weekend Karen, Rosey, and I drove to Southampton, where I met another boy named Carl.

When I returned from Southampton, no one in my house told me Steven had called. I had deliberately put Steven out of my head by then. I had grown irritated by his lack of initiative. He had visited me for months, asked me for my phone number, hinted many, many times that he was going to take me on a date, and never had. My weekend trip to Southampton was just what I needed to get him out of my head for good. I met Carl on the beach. He was forward and direct. When he asked me if he could take me out when he came to Queens, I immediately accepted. Coincidentally, Carl's grandmother lived only a few blocks from me.

By the middle of my first date with Carl, I had already decided it would be our last. Unbeknownst to me, Carl had invited his friend Billy along on the date so he and I could drink. Billy was to act as our designated driver. Neither of them knew it, but I wasn't a drinker. Carl took full advantage of the fact that he didn't have to drive, and got drunk. He was loud sober, and was even more boisterous when he was intoxicated. Carl could never have known that obnoxious boys turned my stomach. By the time he ordered his second drink, I knew I'd never see him again.

Boys like Carl were the reason I liked boys like Steven. And so when Steven showed up at the deli a few weeks later, and asked me how Southampton was, my interest in him resumed. Steven explained that he had called my house and spoken to my brother. I told Steven I never got the message and apologized for not getting back to him. He asked me out on a date that day, and I gladly accepted.

Steven introduced me to his family soon after we met. His family was tight-knit. His mother and father were pleasant, and both made me feel welcome in their modest home. His younger sister Linda was short, perky, and had a wide grin. She too opened her arms to me when we met. His two older brothers and their wives went out of their way to be kind to me as well. I felt embraced by them all. I quickly fell in love with their apparent togetherness. It was common to find them all -- mother, father, sister, brothers and sisters-in-law -- eating dinner at the kitchen table every night. The family felt cohesive, and I liked that very much.

Within a few short months I found myself blending well into this seemingly harmonious family dynamic, and surprisingly even planning my wedding. It was impossible for me not to fall in love with Steven and his family, so different from my own. These people appeared comfortable with needing one another. My mother-in- law was the kind of woman who catered to her children because she wanted to, not because she felt like she had to. She didn't mind whipping up last-minute meals to satisfy the belly of one of her sons, or racing to the bank for them before it closed. Her only teenage daughter owned diamonds and furs, and drove a brand-new car. Her generosity was palpable, and that vibe was one I could not help but gravitate toward.

It was the most peculiar time in my life thus far. As one aspect of my life began to unfold like a fairy tale, a much deeper, darker facet of me thrashed about. As I continued to progress in my physical world, my inner world spun wildly out of control. The gap that existed between both of these worlds was immense, and only I could feel it, or even know it existed at all. The vastness between the two contrasting areas of my life brought with it incredible guilt. In quiet moments, I could not escape feeling like a fake. How could I tell anyone my secret? My life looked perfect now.

Full Steam Ahead

For the first time in my life, I felt safe around others. Steven encouraged me to need him, to rely on him, and to even depend on him. At the end of long overwhelming days at various city hospitals, he would suggest that maybe I should just quit nursing school so he could take care of me. Steven wanted a baby right away and told me he preferred that I not work once we were married. "You could always go back to finish school when our kids get older," was what he said.

The woman I am today knows there is no blame to share. I withdrew from nursing school because of many reasons, and none of them had anything to do with my new husband. My compulsive exercise and eating disorders were like maggots to my soul. I felt eaten from the inside out; my obsessions had successfully bored holes through whatever psychological planks were still managing to hold me up. I found it impossible to focus on nursing school, wedding plans, and my obsessions. Still too asleep to ask for help, I let go of the one area of my life I should have clung to, and withdrew from nursing school in my final semester.

Humility is like a blanket now. But my spirit urges me to lift its chin. These days I have found the eyes that can see within. All that has been, has been but divine stepping stones that have helped pave the road back to me. I cannot blame my wounded heart for gravitating toward what felt like love. Nor can I hold my battered heart accountable for letting go of what it believed at the time was weighing it down. Lack of direction, wisdom, and guidance -- along with ghosts of the past -- all help scurry me toward the illusion of a fairy tale. As forgiveness warms the memories of old, I rest in the knowing that in truth, all I have ever been guilty of is wanting to love, as well as to be loved.

With the stressors of nursing school behind me now, I forged on with the plans for my wedding. Like a leaf caught up in the vortex of a tornado, I chased after sequin-encrusted ideas of fancy. It was impossible to stop the winds of my mind from taking me higher. As if every system in me had suddenly been turned on, and was now catapulting me in this new direction, my future life with Steven took off. Everyone around us was happy we were getting married, from my mother and father to his aunts and uncles, and everyone we knew in between. I was enraptured by the feeling of pleasing others.

My parents adored Steven. They welcomed him into our home and made certain to treat him as if he were born into our family. Steven was good at making my parents feel valid. He supported their egos with his compliments as well as his purposeful undivided attention. He gushed over them, as they gushed over him. As I lift a corner of the veil that blankets my self-awareness and look back at what once was, I find myself unafraid of what, many years ago, had me terrified. Although denial and fear at the time were like emotional cement boots, truth found a way to scribble its message on the walls of my soul in spite of its heavy feet. Tickled by truth, I now know that although I smiled widely as we sifted through wedding invitations, deep within the ocean of my heart, I was ambivalent about marrying Steven. Still too burdened by the pains of my past, and still too hurried to keep them buried, I was unable to turn up the volume of my soul. My future looked bright. My present was illuminated and I simply wanted to forget my past. I was tired of feeling negative emotion, and thus, when nudged by unsettling intuitions, I chose to look ahead, but not before I kissed my spirit good night, and tucked it to sleep.

At the time I did not yet see how destructive my obsession with food or exercise was either. All of my friends worried about their weight, and all of my friends dieted. Everywhere I turned I was praised for being thin. I thought all girls obsessed over what foods they could eat and not eat. I thought all girls exercised for hours at a time. In my mind, I assumed my thinking was the norm. I thought it was normal for girls to be what others wanted them to be, and to do whatever it took to stay that way.

As Dust Settles

My son Max was two years old. Enough time had passed for me to realize that Steven and I had made a grave mistake. It all looked so perfect from the outside. Everything that I had ever thought I wanted, I had drawn to myself. I heard myself knowing that I should have been happy. My spirit was unconcerned now with the "outside." My spirit's eyes weren't outside looking in. They were inside looking out. We were a young attractive couple, living in a custom-built home, and had a healthy baby boy. By all accounts I should have been happy, and I knew that.

As I dangle my toes off of a star, I glance down at the cast of characters in the projection I have perceived as life, and cannot help but smile. Truth, when it comes on the wings of wisdom, has a miraculous way of tickling my spirit's funny bone. It all seems so clear now. It all seems so congruent. My life, so synergistic, has been but an illusion, and I, as the subjective observer, have been little more than a masterful puppeteer, unaware that I was pulling strings.

All drawn unto one another for very specific reasons, the cast of characters in my life have all played their parts well. Every interaction, at every intersection, has assisted me climb the emotional ladder that has helped expand the awareness of self, as well as my relation to all that is. My toes dangle themselves often, from this seat in my expanded consciousness, for it is here, no longer attached to the neurotic need to be validated by others, nor affected by the opinions of others, that I find myself the most comfortable these days. Truth is the only thing that can exist in this place. And it is truth that has set me free.

My soul's skin began to seep truth. And as it did, it became more difficult to control the strings of my life. I found myself entertaining thoughts about leaving him. I even somehow found the courage to tell my mother I was considering separating from Steven. But when she told me I had to lie in the bed I had made, I felt pulled back into the role I had created for myself in the land of the material. I did what I could to convey to Steven that I was not happy. I told him we needed marital counseling. I told him that I didn't feel like we were connected. I told him that I felt like all I was to him was a slab of meat, and a housemaid. I told him that I felt like he didn't see me and that when we spoke, and he told me I was crazy, or insinuated that I had no rights to my feelings, that it made me sad. I told him that when he refused to talk to me for hours or days at a time, that it confused me. I told him that no matter how hard I tried to make him happy, he never seemed satisfied, or let me know he appreciated my efforts. I told him that I felt like I was in the marriage on my own, and that I didn't feel like we were a "we." It was just him, his family, and I was simply there to fulfill his needs, whatever they might be, and whenever they might show up.

In spite of how little I understood about myself at the time, I knew that Steven understood himself even less. Deeper, and more terrifying, was the idea that Steven didn't even know he didn't understand himself. Steven, rooted like a 100-year-old maple tree, believed he knew himself well, and was convinced that what he knew was correct, which made everything about what I was sensing wrong in his eyes. From his perspective, I had no right not to be happy. From his vantage point, I owed him. My instincts were right. Steven didn't see me. Unlike me, Steven enjoyed pulling strings.

One mid-afternoon, Steven came home from work. Max was two at the time, and down for his daily nap. Steven was covered in cement dust. He was unconcerned, however. He wanted sex. Still not the owner of my own soul, mind, or body, I did what he wanted me to do. Beneath him, I cried. The tears were heavy. They flowed thickly from the corners of my eyes, and left wide wet track marks on the sides of my cheeks. As Steven lay above me, the razor-sharp emptiness of the world I had created engulfed me. It was everywhere now. Like the moment the feared hurricane finally hits shore, reality tore at my flesh, as my mind flooded with zapping emotions.

As unhappy as I was, it was not my husband's fault. That fact was what stung the deepest. I had wanted this. I had wanted the husband, the baby, and the home. I had wanted the marriage. I had wanted to quit school and end what I perceived at the time to be stressful suffering. This was my way out. This was the role I chose. I wanted to be a wife and a stay-at-home mommy. Anything and everything I had ever heard myself wanting, I had. The problem was that I wasn't wanting what I should have been wanting. My eyes were so accustomed to focusing outside of myself in the realm of physical reality that I had no understanding of my non-physical reality -- my higher self, my essence, my spirit, my soul, my self. I was so wounded by the scars left by the disease of invisibility I internalized as a child that I had no connection to self. Having never had a sense of "self" reflected back to me, my eyes never learned to nurture that part of me; only a mother's eyes could have helped me connect to within. I had no way of knowing that in order to be happy in the physical realm, I first needed to learn to make my self happy on a soul level, in the realm of the non-physical, the place within me only I could reach by way of my emotions and thoughts, the place in me that I was conditioned to deny.

Steven never noticed the tears I wept that afternoon, nor any of the tears that continued to flow thereafter. That afternoon helped me decide that I could not stay married to Steven for very much longer. I decided to tell him I wanted to separate, but just as I made this decision, I discovered I was pregnant.

The Game Changer

My thoughts immediately shifted when I discovered I was pregnant. As my priorities realigned themselves, I learned to let go of ideas about leaving Steven. I wondered if this were God's way of showing me I was wrong for wanting to leave him. There was no way this could have been a coincidence. I told myself I had to accept that I wasn't supposed to leave Steven -- at least not now -- and looked forward to the arrival of my new baby.

When I was five months pregnant with my second child, my obstetrician told me I should consider an abortion. "You don't want this baby," is what he said. "It is going to be born with a severe neural tube defect and die. Why put yourself through that?" His words vacuumed every molecule of oxygen out of my limping body. As the room began to swirl about me, I struggled before him to stay on my feet. "Your AFP test is terribly high. I'm sorry, Mrs. Romano" I called my husband to tell him what the doctor said. I was crying uncontrollably, and needed him to comfort me. Riddled with guilt for wanting to ever leave Steven, I begged God relentlessly for forgiveness. I felt as if God might be punishing me for such un-Catholic thoughts, and hoped beyond hope that something Steven would say or do could help pull me out of the dark hole I was quickly sinking into.

I was desperate now. The gap within, that was the separateness between my programming and my higher truer self, widened. And as it did, I could feel the depth of its gravity at my feet. As if I were clinging to the edges of my sanity, I struggled not to be taken under by the waves of my toxic emotions. I was not equipped for such non-perfectness. I was not stable enough to handle that which was not working out as I had planned. I was not assured enough to be able to control that which was not within my control. I was not mature enough to deal with something as adult like as this. Me? More than ever, I needed someone to be there for me. I reached for the most logical person in my life for that support: my husband, the father of the child I was being asked to kill.

If Steven was distraught over the idea of my having an abortion, I didn't know it. He seemed indifferent to the news, and implied that I was overreacting. The distance between us was so evident; I felt more alone than I ever had. The baby that I carried was alive. It moved freely within me, like a fish in the sea, or a bird in the sky. I couldn't destroy it. I just couldn't.

Desperate, I decided to contact one of the younger doctors from the ob/gyn office I belonged to. I had always felt more at ease around him than I did the older doctors. He was full of bedside manner, and had never made me feel like anything I asked was silly or irrelevant. When we spoke, he urged me to relax. He explained that many times AFP tests were wrong, and that there was a great chance my child was completely healthy. He told me I would need an amniocentesis to rule out any birth defects. When I asked if he would do the test, he agreed.

My daughter Amanda was born four months later, healthy and beautiful. The original doctor was wrong. No one knew why my tests were so off, although I had an inkling. There was no way I could have been certain, but my gut told me my tests were off because I was under so much stress. I came to conclude that cortisol had in some way affected my test results. So grateful my baby was healthy, I kept the truth about my feeling to myself. Riddled with guilt enough to last one thousand lifetimes, I did what I could to pull myself back into my dutiful roles, and praised God for sparing my baby.

When Amanda was four weeks old, and only about eleven pounds, I found a small lump on the right side of her neck. I was bathing her when I first noticed the thumb-sized tumor. My heart stood still when I laid my eyes upon it. Terrified, I had to remind myself to breathe. As if my life had suddenly flashed before my eyes, anxiety shot through me like electricity. Frozen in fear, I again turned to my husband for comfort, and was once again told I was overreacting. "Even if this was cancer, and the baby died, we'd just have another one anyway," were the words he used to comfort me.

The ear nose and throat specialist I took Amanda too was eight months pregnant. After examining Amanda, she told me she thought my baby had non-Hodgkins lymphoma. "If I were you, I wouldn't get too attached to this baby," were the words she chose. My precious baby, dressed in her teeny white lace socks and pink dress lay sleeping soundly upon my shoulder. The pleasing scent of her newborn skin filled my nostrils, as her tiny perfect little body filled my hands. The doctor's comments made me more angry than they did sad or frightened. I could feel myself wanting to spit in her face, or smack her upside her head. This was my baby, whom I already adored, and I was disgusted by what seemed to be her as well as my husband's indifference toward my baby's life.

"Bring your baby back tomorrow. Then we will do a needle aspiration biopsy. That will help me determine whether this tumor is cancerous or not," she continued, as my veins pumped with venom. The following day we arrived at the doctor's office as planned. My mother accompanied Steven and me there. The doctor asked that I not be the one to hold Amanda during the needle biopsy. Afraid my instinct to protect my daughter from pain might hinder the doctor from being able to stick the sharp needle into my baby's neck, she suggested my mother hold the baby, and I wait outside the office. Shaking from adrenaline caused by anxiety, it was difficult to stay upright. When I heard my baby begin to cry out in pain from being stuck with the thick needle, my legs turned to wet spaghetti and I fainted.

The following day the doctor called to tell me the biopsy was negative. She had not found any malignant cells. I was overjoyed. "Don't get too excited, Mrs. Romano. The tumor still has to come out. I want to do surgery within a few days." My patience had worn thin. On my last nerve, I asked if we could postpone the surgery so I could get a second opinion. "It's your baby's life you're playing with," she said. Her comments helped me decide not only to seek out other opinions, but to search for answers on my own as well.

Karen had finished nursing school and was even working toward becoming a nurse practitioner at that time. I asked her to bring over any medical books she had so I could mull over them. Between her arsenal of books and mine, I gathered together a possible diagnosis of my own. In one of our many books I found a section on newborns and various types of birth marks. When I read the section about hemangiomas, I was convinced this is what Amanda had. Hemangiomas appear in one-third of all newborns shortly after birth. They were classified as benign vascular tumors. Essentially, a hemangioma is a mass of blood vessels.

When I found another surgeon, I told him what I thought. He listened intently and then gently advised that the tumor needed to come out regardless of what any needle aspiration had found or not found. My comfortableness with him made deciding to have surgery performed on my baby less difficult than it could have been. After the operation was over, the surgeon, still dressed in his scrubs, asked me to tell him what I thought the tumor was. I told him I thought the tumor was a hemangioma.

"You were right, Mommy. That is exactly what it was, and had I been sure of it, I would not have done the surgery. Hemangiomas are vascular, meaning that there is a very high risk of bleeding when surgery is performed on them. But your baby is fine. She did very well. She is one hundred percent healthy."

After Shock

Shortly after Amanda's surgery, I started experiencing migraine headaches. Before long I also started feeling tightening in my throat, as if I were being choked. At one of my follow up ob/gyn appointments I told the doctor who had performed Amanda's amniocentesis about my symptoms. I was surprised and confused when he suggested I see a therapist. He told me my symptoms were manifestations of anxiety. He said that what I had gone through with Amanda in the past recent months had affected me psychologically and that I needed help to heal the shock it had caused me emotionally. I knew he was right, but all I could feel was more anxiety. My first thoughts were not about me. They were about Steven. I knew he would not understand, and only label me crazy, weak, or overreactionary.

My doctor suggested that I was experiencing some type of post-traumatic stress disorder. He gave me the number of a therapist to call. Afraid of what Steven, or my parents, or his parents might think, I ignored his advice. In the following months, panic began to take over my body. In the middle of the night I would awaken to the thunder of my heart pounding inside my chest, or to blinding, piercing head pain. I developed asthma, as well as eczema, and found it difficult to sleep. My thoughts easily ran away from me. I found it impossible to concentrate or feel calm. My hands shook, my hair fell out, and my skin flared up as if it were on fire. I felt as if I were being poisoned from the inside out, and sentenced to suffer in silence.

I confided in my Uncle Peter's girlfriend, Sandy. I told her about how anxious I had been feeling. A recovering gambling addict, she turned me on to the twelve-step program, which I embraced fully.

I read the material she gave me, and felt that perhaps I was on the right track. Although I was not an alcoholic, or compulsive gambler, I was an addict. Addicted to fear and worry, I absorbed the idea of leaning on a higher power to help me gain control back over my life.

As time progressed, I decided to learn all I could about asthma, eczema, and migraine headaches. When I finally made the connection between negative thinking, anxiety, cortisol, and inflammation, I realized that my body was simply reacting to whatever was going on inside of me emotionally. Approximately four or five years after Amanda was born, I came to believe that I needed to address the unhappiness in my marriage. Just as I began scraping together the courage to once more suggest to Steven that he and I go into couples counseling, I got pregnant for the third time. I wondered if there were a conspiracy brewing somewhere in the cosmos that I wasn't aware of.

This pregnancy was different, however. In spite of all the joy and delight I experienced while being pregnant, in the back of my mind I knew that one day soon, I would need to confront Steven once and for all. After Niccole was born, my body began to fail quickly. My asthma worsened significantly. The allergist who was treating my asthma told me that there was no physical reason for my condition.

"You'd better listen to your body, because your body is listening to you," he said.

The dermatologist I was seeing for my eczema was so perplexed by the bumps on my skin that he ordered a punch hole biopsy of my left hip. A giant butterfly-shaped outbreak on my hip had him flustered. Nothing he was prescribing was working. The biopsy was inconclusive. He said all he could determine was that I was experiencing hive breakouts and he didn't know why. "I think you're probably the only one who really knows why this is all happening to you," he said.

I rushed myself to the allergist one afternoon, gasping for breath. I felt as if there were an elephant sitting on my chest. I couldn't draw breath in, nor could I breathe air out. As if I were breathing air through a thin cocktail straw, my body struggled to survive. Afraid I might die, I called my mother and asked her to watch the kids so I could get to the doctor's office quickly. Once I was there, he immediately started me on an IV of liquid steroids and antibiotic treatments. Angrily the doctor asked me, "Did your husband take the rugs out of your bedroom like I asked him to three years ago?"

Tired, feeling defeated, with my head buried in my lap and my eyes closed, I shook my head slowly side to side, and whispered the word "No."

I was sitting upright in a dark room when Steven arrived at the office with the three kids. He was holding Niccole in his arms when he came to see me in the rear area of the doctor's office. "Mr. Romano, do you remember me telling you to remove the carpets from your bedroom about three years ago?" the doctor asked Steven. I was afraid to look up. Asthma had very much won that day, and I did not feel strong enough to handle Steven's glares. Steven did not answer the doctor's question. All he did was stare at me angrily, annoyed at the idea that I had perhaps ratted him out, and in some way placed blame on him.

"Just so you know, your wife is breathing with less than twenty percent lung capacity. Do you understand how dangerous this is, Mr. Romano? Your wife almost died today. If she hadn't gotten herself here, or if she had instead taken a nap, she might not have woken up. Do you get that?" The doctor continued to press Steven for a response.

"Yeah, yeah, yeah -- okay, Doc. I hear ya ... I hear ya....Okay, so I have to rip the rugs up. No big deal," Steven said.

Down but Not Out

It took another year for me to find the courage to confront Steven once more. My doctors were right. There was something wrong, and I needed to finally address it. I was tired of suffering in silence and having my body pay the price. I was tired of pretending to be happy when I wasn't. I was tired of having sex with a man who had no feelings for me. I was tired of cleaning a house that felt more like a prison than a home, my home. I was tired of feeling like I owed Steven and his family for building us a house I never asked for. And most of all, I was tired of me ignoring me.

When I told Steven I wanted to go into couples counseling, he reacted worse than I thought he would. Over the next few days he found ways to express his displeasure with my desire. When he came home from work, he ignored me, darted angry looks my way over dinner, and slammed kitchen cabinet doors before bed. One time he turned over our furniture like a rhino, slammed his fists on the counter, slapped a dish soap bottle across the room as he yelled, "So you want a divorce, Lisa? Is that what you want huh? You want a divorce, Lisa?" as if to threaten me with the idea, in front of our children.

Tempted to give in to his temper for the sake of my children, I often found myself questioning how far I wanted this to go. Steven was not aware enough to not use our children as pawns against me. It became obvious quickly that my children were going to suffer at the hands of his lack of self-control, and that I was going to be the one blamed for the trauma. I needed to remind myself often that all I wanted was a better marriage, and that I was not the one threatening him with a divorce. I simply needed to know our life together had a chance of getting better. What we had was killing me.

On the afternoon I had finally decided to make an appointment with a marriage counselor, my mother-in-law called to tell me that her daughter Linda had stage four cancer. Linda was going to need nursing care, and she called to enlist my aid. Once more, like a magnet at work sorting through my list of priorities, my life shifted sharply. As always, my needs took last place on the totem pole, and I, as usual, raced to the rescue.

The need to help Linda consumed me. In the recent years she and I had stopped speaking. A conversation I had had with her husband years prior had been twisted into a diabolical knot. I was quoted as saying things I hadn't. Linda unfortunately refused to listen to my side of the story and impulsively decided to cut me out of her life. Her decision tore through her family and me like a laser. My relationships with her brothers, their parents, and her were never the same. I ached for many years over the unnecessary chaos her choice produced, but eventually learned to accept that which I could not change. I knew in my heart I wasn't guilty of saying the things she presumed I had.

I raced to Linda's house the day my mother-in-law called to ask me for my help. It was the first time in seven years that Linda and I spoke. For me, however, the slate had been wiped clean. All I could think about at the time was saving this young 28-year-old mommy with two small children from death. For days I researched alternative cancer therapies in the hopes that something, anything, might help Linda. The doctors had told her and her family that there was nothing more they could do for her. Her disease had progressed too far.

Linda had been diagnosed with adrenal cortical carcinoma. Cancer had spread to both her lungs, and to her abdominal cavity, and had also been found in various lymph nodes. The first time I saw Linda, shock fell over me. She was no longer the vibrant young girl I once knew. Her skin was grey, and she had thick facial hair along the sides of her face. Her abdomen was distended, and her breathing was evidently labored. Her voice was weak, and her arms and hands seemed frail. My heart burst open like a dam when my eyes fell upon her. The sight of her children, one on each side of her, nearly floored me with grief. I knew instantly, the moment I looked at Linda, that she might not get to see her two little angels grow up.

When I returned home that night after spending the evening with Linda and her children, I felt drained. The number for the marriage counselor I had intended to call earlier was still on my kitchen island next to the phone. I stood and gazed upon it for about five minutes before I slid to my knees and began to cry. I cried not only for Linda, her babies, and my in-laws, but for myself as well. I cried because of all the time Linda and I had lost. I cried because her children didn't know me or my children. I cried because I was angry that she had gotten sick just as I had found the courage to confront my marital problems. I cried because I felt obligated to once again put others' needs ahead of my own. I cried because I was tired. I cried because I was scared as well as sad. But most of all, I cried because I felt so guilty for wanting more than what I had.

Spirit is with me now. And as I tap away at these lettered keys, I am softly reminded to be kind to my self as I remember the past, for it is still far too easy for the woman I am to cloak herself in guilt unnecessarily, even all these years later. Yes, I was angry that Linda got sick when she did. And yes, I did feel guilty for feeling that way. Rampages of emotion were common back then, and sometimes identifying any of them was impossible. Sometimes all I could do was cry. So overwhelmed by feelings I did not know how to feel, assimilate, or name, weeping was the way my body relieved some of the pressure the onslaught of negative emotions caused.

I sat upon my cold ceramic white and black tiled kitchen floor for what seemed like hours, just crying. My mind tossed and turned as it struggled to survive the volleys between anger, sadness, frustration, shame -- and of course, guilt. When it felt like I had finally cried my eyes dry, I stayed seated upon the floor until I was clear about what direction I was headed. I decided that I would do what I could to help

Linda. I came to convince myself that God must have had a plan. I wondered if Linda's cancer was the way God was going to bring us all back together, including Steven and me. I thought that perhaps my husband's sister's disease would wake him up, and maybe through the storm of what was ahead, our marriage would be strengthened. I believed all of these things with all my heart, so much so that I dedicated my life to Linda and her family, convinced that only good could come from doing so.

After about six months of helping my mother-in-law care for Linda daily, I decided I could no longer continue doing so. The fantasies I had had about Linda's cancer being the vehicle God was going to use to bring about healing in this family was just that -- a fantasy. Nothing good that I thought might happen did. In fact, things only worsened. The final straw for me came the one night I revisited Linda late in the evening. She was now on a blood thinner that needed to be injected two times a day. I was the one giving her the shots. That evening, I was feeling tired. My asthma had been flaring up, and I was having trouble sleeping. I was also growing aware of how little attention I had been paying to my own household chores as the result of spending so much time taking care of Linda, her house, and her children. I was upset when I realized how little time I had been spending alone with my own children, and was unhappy when I realized I had little patience for them when we were alone at home. I could not ignore how my children's lives had been impacted by my decision to dive into caring for Linda. As usual, my all-or-nothing personality had whipped my butt good, and left me even more drained than ever.

To make matters worse, Keith, the oldest sibling to Steven and Linda, treated me with disrespect, in spite of my efforts to help his family care for Linda. Keith had stopped speaking to me years prior, since I confronted him about his relationship with one of our female customers that frequented our store-- a relationship that was making our very good employee so awkward she told me she might have to quit. Keith went out of his way to make me feel uncomfortable in his presence every time he visited his sister while I was there. But the night I went to give Linda her blood thinner injection, and he sat next to her on the couch, and huffed and puffed and obnoxiously turned his head to avoid looking in my direction to make it clear he was disgusted by my presence, I drew the line. In that moment, I was done.

I called Linda the next day to discuss Keith's behavior. I knew I was going out on a limb by confronting a personal truth of mine, but I felt as if I had no other choice. If I were going to go on caring for Linda, my feelings were going to have to be considered. Taking care of her was trying enough, without being treated in such a ridiculous way. I hated that I was putting Linda on the spot, but there was no way I could go on taking care of her while she ignored the way her brother treated me. That night, as I knelt upon my knee and searched Linda's flesh for a new injection site and her brother rolled his eyes when he looked at me, and she allowed it, I realized I didn't matter to either of them. In my mind, I began to understand that I was just a tool. I was there to fill a need. Who I was, was irrelevant. And all the tears I had cried over this young woman, and all the dreams I had had about bringing this family back together were for nothing.

Around the time that I stopped caring for Linda, she decided to forgo the alternative therapies I had taught her, and instead chose to go with traditional chemotherapy. Her doctors were surprised at how well she had been doing, and told her and her family that she was now strong enough to handle chemotherapy. Linda passed away about six months later. An infection in her leg led to pneumonia. Ultimately her liver failed, and Linda died. The night of her death was excruciating for us all. In spite of the cockamamie bullshit that filled the air among those of us who loved Linda, gathered around her bedside in the hospital, we were all one, unified by grief.

Round Two

Life stood still for a while after Linda died. My heart felt as if someone had nailed its feet to the ground. The reality of her death was incomprehensible at times. The idea that her children would grow without knowing her choked air from my lungs. It all seemed so unnatural, out of rhythm, and void of rhyme. What was should not have been. Her death not was not only disillusioning; it was enlightening as well. More than ever, I wanted to live, and I wanted to live well.

It took me many weeks after Linda's death to remind Steven that I wanted us to start marital counseling. I was full of fear when I confronted him, because I was certain he'd use his sister's death as a weapon of control against me. The day I confronted Steven, he accused me of being selfish and told me I did not have my priorities straight. He told me I had no right to feel the way I felt. He said I should be grateful I lived the way I did, and that I had three healthy children. He told me customers at our store told him I should kiss his feet when he came home at the end of day. He told me he could get any woman he wanted, and that any other woman would be happy to have him in her life.

This behavior was typical of Steven. He liked using guilt and shame against me whenever I tried to address a topic that he didn't want to discuss. But this time his manipulative tactics did not work. Too tired, too sad, too depressed, and entirely too angry to care what he thought about me anymore, I pulled the number to the therapist out from behind the phone and said, "Either you call to make the appointment, or I will. But you need to know, I'm not playing around with you anymore. I am not happy, and something must change if our marriage is going to survive."

After a few more temper tantrums, Steven agreed to see a counselor with me. On the drive home that night after our first therapy session,

Steven was irate. He was angry at how open I was with our therapist. He felt threatened by the therapist's empathy for my feelings about how unhappy I was with the state of our marriage. I was honest and told her I felt used, unappreciated, and more like a piece of meat in bed than a woman. I told her that my husband never considered my feelings in any decisions and often ignored me. I told her that he called me crazy, said I was a flake, and made fun of me whenever I didn't agree with him. I told her I was tired of our loveless sex life and the disconnection between us. I told her I needed for things to change. I wanted to feel like Steven and I were on the same page, and like he was in my corner, instead of feeling like I always had to keep my hands up around him. By the time our first session ended, I admitted that I didn't feel emotionally, physically, or sexually safe around Steven, and if things didn't change, I was going to leave him.

On the drive home from that first therapy session, Steven drove at high speeds, zipping fiercely around corners. He banged his fists on the steering wheel, his face contorted with rage, and yelled angrily about how I had embarrassed him. "Everything is about your feelings, Lisa; your feelings, Lisa; your feelings, your feelings," he said, mocking me as if to suggest my feelings were invalid. I was afraid Steven might hurt us both that night, and I wasn't certain it would not have been unintentional.

Steven refused to go to another therapy session with MaryAnn. He said I embarrassed him in front of her, and told me my feelings were ridiculous. He said he had no interest in going to talk to a stranger about such personal issues. He said only weak people need therapy. He said he didn't need any help. He said he was happy, and had no intention of changing. He said that what I wanted out of a marriage didn't exist. He told me I was ungrateful, selfish, negative, and too sensitive. After I begged him to change his mind, I made the decision to go without him. When I arrived alone, MaryAnn told me that his absence spoke volumes, and that my presence there alone spoke just as loudly.

I continued to see MaryAnn weekly without Steven. A few months into our sessions, she announced that she was moving, and referred me to another therapist, named Ed. When I told Steven MaryAnn was no longer going to be our therapist and that she had given me the number to a new one, he laughed.

"You're really going to go through with this therapy shit, Lisa? Are you serious? I thought you'd give up by now. But hey, if you feel crazy, then maybe you do need therapy," he said. I called to make an appointment with Ed the following morning.

The Home Stretch

"So tell me ... who is Lisa?" was the first question Ed asked.

Sitting directly across from him in a shoebox-sized office, I said, "Well, I … umm ... I am a wife and a mother, and I am the head of security at my children's school. I am a member of the PTA, and my husband and I own and manage our own business," I replied.

"I didn't ask you what you did. I asked you who you were," he answered.

If my soul had ears, they were listening now. As if a trumpet had been blown, the spirit that I had so often forced to sleep began to awaken. There were gaps, spaces, crevices, holes, even oceans within, which kept the various facets of me foreign to one another. My body, mind, and soul were so detached from one another; each lived separate experiences within. When Ed made it clear what he was asking, for the first time ever in my life perhaps, my body and my mind, as well as my soul, were all listening. Ed's first question had sucked me into the now.

"What is your highest level of education?"

"I went to college for nursing," I answered.

"Did you graduate?" he asked.

"No."

"Well, then -- you're not a nurse, are you?" he continued.

"No, I suppose I'm not."

"You suppose you're not, or you know you're not?"

"No, no -- I know I am not a nurse," I said, as I began to grow fidgety in my seat. Ed's questions were direct, to the point, and no-nonsense. In this space between myself and Ed, there was no room for denial or evasiveness. Ed meant business, and I, at the moment, was his business. It was peculiar to have someone's one hundred percent attention. For the first time in my life, I felt that I was being taken seriously, that I was being heard -- and most importantly, that I was being seen.

"Why are you here?"

"My husband says I am crazy," I replied.

"Do you think you're crazy, Lisa?" he asked.

"I'm not sure. All I know is I'm not happy."

"What would make you happy?"

"I don't feel like my husband and I are on the same page. When I try to talk to him about how I feel, he always tells me I have no right to feel the way I do. He tells me that life shouldn't be about the way I feel. He tells me I should be happy I live in the big house that I have, and that he doesn't cheat on me, and that we have three healthy children. He makes me feel like I don't matter, and yet, I worry every day about how to make his life easier. And when something is bothering him, I am always there for him. So when he calls me names like whacko, psycho, or when he ignores me or says that I am a negative person, it hurts. I feel like he is a stranger to me, but yet he is so happy with the way things are. So I wonder if maybe I am crazy sometimes," I said.

Ed sat quietly as he scribbled notes on a long yellow legal pad. It was easy for me to cite the extensive lists of things I didn't like about Steven and our marriage. It was all I had thought about for many years. On some level, I was proud that I could answer Ed's last question, and then he said, "I didn't ask you what made you unhappy, Lisa. I asked you what would make you happy."

Ed placed his pen on his desk, his pad next to his pen, and folded his hands in his lap. "We have a lot of work to do with you, Lisa," he whispered softly. Perplexed, but highly curious as well, I felt as if every nerve cell in my body was standing at attention. I wanted more of whatever this was. In the short moments that Ed and I had spent together, I could feel the fog in my mind begin to clear. As if Ed were a dust pan and broom, his questions began to make me understand as well as believe that it was possible to untangle the tremendous knot of thoughts in my mind. I also understood that this man was not going to leave any stones unturned. This process was not going to be easy. It would require great courage for me to see it through. Like a lion scratching at his cage, eager to be set free, Ed's questions were like the keys to the lock that had kept me behind bars.

"Is there any alcoholism in your family, Lisa?"

"My parents don't drink," I replied.

"Listen to my question, and answer the question I am asking. Is there any history of alcoholism in your family?"

"Yes. Both sets of my grandparents were alcoholics, and both of my mother's brothers are alcoholics too, but my parents aren't alcoholics," I said.

"I don't remember asking you if your parents were alcoholics," Ed pushed, to make sure I understood I was still not answering the question he had asked.

"Yes, there is alcoholism in my family," I said as I smiled widely.

My mind felt like it was dancing on hot coals. Ed's direct approach was teaching me to let go of my need to worry about what other people thought. Ed was not there to judge me. Nor was he there to allow me to fall into the trap of judging myself. He simply wanted me to get clear about the facts, and assist me in seeing things for what they were, without a neurotic compulsion to sugarcoat them. If Ed was going to help me, he was going to need to find a way to get me to figure out who I was, minus the facades. I didn't know where I might end up, but I knew I liked feeling that I was on the right road.

I'm Not Crazy --
I'm Just Co-dependent

The question and answer session between Ed and me quickly became a sort of game. I felt as if his spirit were joking with mine. I had great respect for his keen ability to help me see so swiftly the inappropriateness of my thoughts. In less than forty-five minutes, Ed was able to turn my mind around at least one hundred and eighty degrees, in a direction that felt as if it were actually calling me forth.

"I've got some good news and some bad news for you, Lisa," Ed said as he knotted his fingers behind his head and leaned back in his chair. "The good news is you're not crazy. The bad news is you are, however, severely co-dependent. Your family has a long history of alcoholism. Your parents are adult children of alcoholics, which is why they were attracted to one another in the first place. More often than not, adult children are unaware of how deeply affected they are by their parents' alcoholism. In short, you were raised by adult children of alcoholics, and you need to learn as much as you can about how alcoholism has indirectly affected you. Your life is the result of the way you think, and your thinking is the result of your childhood programming and conditioning, and your programming is the result of whatever your parents' programming was. So, in order for you to truly figure this mess out, you'll need to go back to where you began. Are you willing to take that journey?"

The First Step Home

I left Ed's office that day feeling awake. It was still early in my journey, but at least I felt like I had found a path I could follow out of the depraved forest of thoughts I was currently living in. Ed told me he wanted me to pick up a few books to help get me going on my journey toward self-discovery. He suggested the books *Co-dependent No More* and *The Art of Letting Go*, both by Melodie Beattie. That afternoon, I didn't walk to the bookstore. I ran to the bookstore.

The first few pages of *Co-dependent No More* spooked me. It was as if I were reading a book that had been written just for my sake -- its honesty, truth, vigor, and clarity were almost too much for my mind to handle. Instinctively I understood that if I kept reading this book, I would finally understand who I was. I felt as one might feel when asked if they were interested in meeting a parent they had never known. I wondered if I'd like who I found, and struggled with ideas of the unknown. If I kept reading this book, and others about co-dependency, things in my life would change. They would have to, because the things that I discovered would change me.

I absorbed Melodie Beattie's two books like a dry sponge would water. Until I read her books, I had no inkling of how thirsty I really was. Ed was right. I was severely co-dependent. I was lost inside a world that had been defined by two well-intentioned adult children of alcoholics, whose own lives had been directly affected by alcohol addiction. What I thought and believed about my world was built on their dysfunctional belief systems. My parents could never have known how faulty their belief systems were. My brother, sister, and I had been affected by alcoholism -- indirectly, but affected nonetheless.

As if my mind were being cranked open like an aluminum can, these books shed light on areas of my life that might have stayed dark forever had I never learned about them. The information I gathered, along with my weekly sessions with Ed, helped me maintain my focus in the days ahead. Ed helped me understand that in order for me to be truly healthy one day, I would have to understand my self from the inside out. He made me appreciate how little Steven had to do with how unhappy I was. My problems began the day I was conceived by a nineteen-year-old old teenage girl whose mother and father were both alcoholics, not the day I chose to quite nursing school to marry Steven.

I begged my husband to come with me to meet Ed. Steven was as co-dependent as I was. He was dependent on me, and I was dependent on him. In order for either of us to be healthy, we'd have to face this emotional disease head-on. I believed with all my heart that if Steven opened his mind to what I was trying to accomplish, we could rise above all that had been. I was clear about my goal. After reading *Co-dependent No More,* I was certain what I had to do. It became my passion to break the cycle of co-dependency that had plagued my family for generations. I loved my children too deeply to not take this journey.

Steven refused to see Ed. He did, however, agree to see another marriage counselor in the area, named Alice. Steven and I went to see Alice as a couple. Within a few months of couples counseling Alice asked me if it would be all right for her to start having sessions with Steven alone. "As far as I can tell, Lisa, you're clear about what you want. You want your marriage to work, but it has to change in order for it to survive. And I can tell that you are willing to do whatever it takes to see that it does survive. I'm not sure, however, if your husband is as willing to do whatever it takes to have a healthy marriage. So, I'd like a few sessions with him alone to help me figure out where his head is at," she said.

A few weeks later, my kitchen phone rang. It was Alice. "Hi, Lisa, do you have a minute?" she asked.

"Sure," I said, eager to hear what she had to say.

"After spending time with Steven, I need to tell you that he is not wiling to change. He is not willing to learn about co-dependency. He has no interest in changing any of his ways, and in fact is enraged that you are not happy, and expect him to change at all. In his mind you owe him gratitude. In his view, you are selfish and unrealistic. He insists that he thinks you are crazy for even wanting to go into therapy. He doesn't think there is anything wrong with him, or with the way he treats you."

Tears had already begun to flow by the end of Alice's third sentence. I realized that Steven and I were at a stalemate and that his inability to meet me halfway meant I was going to have to make some serious decisions about the rest of my life. By then I had learned enough about co-dependency to realize that I could not change anyone else but me, and that I couldn't save my marriage all by myself. "What now, Alice? I don't want to get a divorce."

"Lisa, you can't stop now. You're on the right track, and you can't go back. And if you did, all that you have learned so far will have been for nothing. You have a giant little boy on your hands," she said.

The Road Back To Me

My kids were sitting on our couch. They were watching *Rugrats* on Nickelodeon. Steven had just come home from work. He had had a session with Alice earlier that afternoon. He looked angry. His keys made a loud clanging noise when he tossed them on the counter. He ignored me when I said hello. My back was to him. I was stirring tomato sauce in a pan. We were having spaghetti for dinner that night. I savored the moment. We were all together. However, everything was about to change. I could feel it.

I was getting ready to drain the spaghetti when Steven's voice cracked the deafening silence between us. "Alice said I don't have to change just because you want me to. She said I didn't have to do anything I didn't want to. She also said I have a right to feel any way I want. So guess what? I'm not gonna change. That's my decision."

Ed had suggested that I learn to hold on to myself whenever I was around someone I feared. I practiced not reacting to what Steven was saying, and instead chose to just let it sink in. "So -- so what are you gonna do now, wiseass?" Steven asked, as he stood eerily close, almost whispering in my ear. I turned to look him straight in the eye. I stood still for a few moments, as the steam from the pasta that was rising out of the sink moistened the back of my t-shirt. My eyes locked on his; I searched for a hint of the man that I knew existed somewhere behind his eyes. But all I found was rage.

I glanced over at my three babies sitting there on our maroon leather couch. They had grown tired of listening to their father and mother bicker. These days, they lost themselves in lands of make- believe on cable television. Their blank stares tore at my heart. I could no longer ignore the reality of what I had done. In that moment, I knew I needed to put the brakes on the momentum of my life.

"You know what's gonna happen if you keep this shit up, Lisa? We're gonna end up getting a divorce because you won't drop this crazy bullshit of yours. Everything is about your feelings, your feelings, your feelings. Ya think most people are happy these days? Nobody is happy these days, Lisa. What you want doesn't even exist. But I am warning you ... if you don't stop going to this whacko Ed, and if you don't stop reading these self-help books, we're gonna wind up getting a divorce. Is that what you want, Lisa? You want to get divorced, huh, huh, huh? Well, do ya?" Steven prodded, his voice growing more intimidating with every syllable.

As if my spirit were speaking, I replied, "No, Steven I don't want a divorce. I need a divorce." I stared deeply into his milk-chocolate-brown eyes. "Alice is right. You don't have to change. That is your right. But I have rights too. And I have the right to want more out of a marriage. I know now that I cannot change you. I was wrong to try. I am sorry. I am sorry I am not what you want me to be. And I am sorry, but you are not what I want you to be. I am sorry I enabled you. I am sorry I worried so much about what you thought about me. I should have not made you responsible for my happiness. I was wrong to expect you to make me feel worthy. It was never your job to give me what I should have been able to give my self.

Steven didn't know it, but I was saying goodbye. Steven stood there looking puzzled. He was not used to my being so calm and clear. The years leading up to this point were drizzled in frustration and, many times, in tears. On that day, however, I discovered that I had no more tears to cry. I was done. As if a giant wind had blown all my feelings for Steven out a back door, any loving emotion I had ever had for him was gone.

I called the kids to the dinner table. They loved spaghetti, and I loved watching them eat it. Steven sat down to eat with the kids. He was quiet, and only grunted a few times when one of the kids asked him to pass a napkin. I was surprised at how peaceful I felt. This would most likely be our last meal together as a family, although I was sure Steven was convinced I was bluffing.

Ed and Melodie Beattie were wonderful teachers. I learned the lessons they had taught me well. Ed told me not to expect things to change overnight. He said that it had taken me a long time to get to where I was, and that it would take a long time to get to where I wanted to go. He also said every new journey begins with a first step.

As I sat there at the white Formica kitchen table, and watched everyone slurp their spaghetti, I did so quietly without saying a word, as an observer, detached from the dynamic I had created. I could sense the powerful pull of inertia within me, slamming the brakes on the runaway train that had become my life. I no longer felt like a puppet on a string. I felt more like a fly on the wall now, or a caterpillar about to burst out of her cocoon. I didn't know where I was going, but I did know I had to go.

The road back to me has been long. Many times I have stumbled along the way. Often I felt so overwhelmed by fear, doubt, and guilt that I considered turning back. In the beginning I felt like I had stepped into an abyss. My three small children clinging to my apron strings compounded my worries. This was not an adventure I would be taking alone. The determination I had to break the cycle of co-dependency in my life carried me forward in my darkest moments. In times when I found myself haunted by loneliness, doubt, shame, and guilt, I reminded myself that my children were learning from me. I had to face the demons and put them to rest if I were to be able to spare my children from the horrific illusions of co-dependency in their lives. The love and respect I had for their future was the light that lit the path on the road back to me.

CPSIA information can be obtained
at www.ICGtesting.com
Printed in the USA
BVHW081441270620
582380BV00002B/170

9 780578 102689